· Cabins · Condos · Mountain retreats · Seaside cottages

Maintaining a VACATION HOME

A Practical Guide To: Seasonal Maintenance · Opening and Closing · Guest Procedures · Pest Control · Repairs

Steve Grooms

Creative Publishing international

CHANHASSEN, MINNESOTA
www.creativepub.com

Creative Publishing international

Copyright © 2006
Creative Publishing international, Inc.
18705 Lake Drive East
Chanhassen, Minnesota 55317
1-800-328-3895
www.creativepub.com

Printed at R.R. Donnelley

10 9 8 7 6 5 4 3 2 1

President/CEO: Ken Fund
Vice President/Retail Sales & Marketing: Kevin Haas

Executive Editor: Bryan Trandem

Author: Steve Grooms
Editor: Jerri Farris
Art Director: David Schelitzche
Assistant Managing Editor: Tracy Stanley
Photo Acquisitions Editor: Julie Caruso
Production Manager: Linda Halls

CONTENTS

CHAPTER 1
VACATION HOME BASICS

CHAPTER 2
VACATION HOMES AND WHAT MAKES THEM DIFFERENT

CHAPTER 3
DIFFERENT TYPES OF VACATION HOMES

CHAPTER 4
OPENING WEEKEND

CHAPTER 5
CRITTERS

CHAPTER 6
NETWORKING WITH THE LOCAL COMMUNITY

CHAPTER 7
GUESTS

CHAPTER 8
SUMMERTIME MAINTENANCE

CHAPTER 9
SHORELINE AND LAWN MAINTENANCE

CHAPTER 10
SEASON'S END SHUTDOWN

CHAPTER 11
PROJECTS

Library of Congress Cataloging-in-Publication Data

Grooms, Steve.
  Maintaining a vacation home : a practical guide to seasonal
maintenance, opening and closing, guest procedures, pest control,
repairs / by Steve Grooms.
    p. cm.
  Summary: "Shows readers how to put a vacation home to rest at the end
of a holiday season, to protect it from the elements that can ruin it,
how to open it up at the start of the vacation season, and time-saving
ways to maintain a seasonal home through the vacation weeks"--Provided
by publisher.
  ISBN 1-58923-250-X (soft cover)
  1. Vacation homes--Maintenance and repair--Amateurs' manuals. I. Title.

  TH4817.G76 2006
  643'.25--dc22
                        2005030250

CHAPTER 1

VACATION HOME BASICS

A T A PARTY MANY YEARS AGO, I MET A MAN WHO HAD SPENT THE PREVIOUS WEEKEND LOOKING FOR RECREATIONAL PROPERTY THAT HE AND HIS WIFE COULD AFFORD.

"It's my lifelong dream to own a vacation home," he said, oozing enthusiasm.

"It is my lifelong dream," I said, "to not own a vacation home."

"What do you mean?"

"Think about it. After a week of work, you get in your car and drive for five hours to arrive at your dream home in its remote location. You walk in to find that squirrels have been nesting in the sofa, and now bits of stuffing are scattered all over. You spend all day Saturday and much of Sunday repairing screens, mowing the lawn and splitting wood. You drive back home Sunday in heavy traffic, feeling more exhausted than you were on Friday. And if you're really unlucky, next weekend you get to do it all over again!"

"It doesn't have to be that way," said the would-be cabin owner, sounding a little petulant.

"If you own a second home," I went on, "you have two driveways to maintain. Two lawns to mow. Two plumbing systems to keep flowing. Two roofs to keep watertight. You've got twice as many windows to wash. If your home is on a lake, you probably have to put the dock in and take it out each season. Just when you think you've got the place in good shape, along comes a windstorm that drops a red pine through the roof of the garage. No, if the Good Lord is kind to me, I might be lucky enough to never own a vacation home!"

My new acquaintance seemed to find me more annoying than clever, and he moved off to talk to someone else.

I thought of him several years later. That man would have gotten a laugh out of the spectacle of my grand project to install a water system at my north woods cabin.

The cabin my family bought didn't have a plumbing system, so I built one. I undertook this project in late June during a stretch of monsoon weather. It rained all day and during most of the night for ten days. The only way I could build a water system was to wriggle around on my back in the muck of the crawl space. Because I was looking up, spiders, insulation and woody debris kept falling in my eyes. Meanwhile, the local mosquitoes were busy taking samples of my blood.

Vacation homes come in all varieties—from wilderness cabins to luxury condo villages, like this one.

The man I had offended with my sarcastic vision of cabin life might have gotten a chuckle out of seeing me scooting around in all that slimy red clay, but then again he might have noticed something else: I was grinning like a kid on Christmas morning. I was having fun.

TRENDS

Many people are buying recreational property now, a boom that has several origins.

Some observers note that the bloom is off the early promise of suburbs. After World War II, many middle-class families fled the major cities in favor of the relatively open and bucolic environment of suburbs. It was considered a way of having the best of both worlds. Suburban dwellers enjoyed "nature" in the form of lawns, gardens, and boulevard trees, yet they were close to the cities so they could commute to good jobs. Then about once a year, suburbanites took a two- or three-week vacation, staying at some resort or cabin in undeveloped country.

That pattern has largely broken down. Suburban houses don't seem much more "natural" than central city homes. They have larger lawns, but beyond that they hardly offer the restorative effect of recreation in an undeveloped area. At the same time, the traditional two- or three-week summer vacation has disappeared in favor of several shorter vacations.

These changes leave many families hungry for time spent in beautiful, undeveloped places. Increasingly, families are finding that owning a vacation property offers them the chance to make a good living in a metro area while still being able to duck out frequently for a few days of relaxation.

Second homes are increasingly popular for financial reasons, too. Many investors have become disillusioned with the stock market. After the swoon of stock values late in the 20th century, real estate has become popular as a safer place to place investment funds. And while home values have soared, recreational real estate has increased in value at an even steeper rate. The baby boom generation is more affluent and mobile than any of the generational cohorts that preceded it. Boomers are now snapping up lakefront, mountain and seashore property.

Technology has had an impact as well. Improved highways have made vacation property closer (in terms of travel time) than it was decades ago. The rise of the Internet has made it easier for people to work on laptop computers in remote areas, relaying their work to the office. Advances in telecommunications have made it easier to be "on vacation" and yet keep in touch with developments at work.

About 15 percent of recent real estate purchases have been second homes, many of them considered recreational properties. Every state in the Union has some lands considered desirable for recreational use, but the most desirable recreational lands are concentrated in mountains or near water of some sort. For many would-be buyers, a critical requirement is that the recreational property

Many vacation homes use unique building materials that may offer new maintenance challeges....

not be too far away from the primary home. The median distance driven to recreational property is 185 miles. Americans are said to own over 5 million vacation homes. Interest in recreational property has spiked in recent years.

THE DARK TRUTH ABOUT SECOND HOMES

Recreational property is a wonderful thing. Almost everyone who enjoys nature has dreamed of owning a charming cottage in the woods, up in the mountains, by the lake or perhaps along the shore of some ocean.

There is, unfortunately, a pesky difference between dreams and reality.

When people dream about owning a second home in an undeveloped area, they picture themselves with their feet up, possibly listening to music while enjoying a frosty glass of lemonade. They don't dream about waging a territorial war with skunks over ownership of the space under the toolshed. They don't dream about backed-up septic tanks. They don't dream about driving up a dark driveway, only to find that a 50-foot tree has fallen across it.

Owning a second home brings many extra responsibilities and chores, and there isn't usually a whole lot of time to do those chores. When you conduct a home improvement project in your primary home, you usually have the luxury of choosing the ideal time for the project. Vacation home maintenance is often done on an emergency basis during a quick weekend visit, and that kind of chore can quickly sap the fun out of a getaway weekend.

A WIDE RANGE OF ATTITUDES

People have very different attitudes about the toil they put into sprucing up their recreational property. Let's consider the cases of two people I've known.

Nobody enjoyed working on a cabin more than my neighbors, John and Judy. John and Judy approached cabin life as one big delightful list of chores. They spent virtually all of their time building, painting, repairing, improving or replacing things. When they ran out of projects to do at their rustic cabin, John and Judy began to build a new one. They worked like beavers for three summers creating that dream cabin.

When the new cabin was finished, John and Judy tried to enjoy themselves, but they never seemed to have the knack. Two years

after finishing construction, they sold it to some college kids from Wisconsin. It seemed to me that they got bored when they ran out of improvement projects.

SOME PEOPLE ARE JUST THE OPPOSITE

My family spent a lot of time at the cabin of a couple whose passion was to enjoy their cabin while minimizing work there. Eleanor used cabin time to read good books. Bob's favorite position at the cabin was prone. When feeling more ambitious, Bob would sit upright in a big stuffed chair with a martini in one hand and his pipe in the other. In the six years our family shared time with Bob and Eleanor, I never saw Bob attempt a maintenance or improvement project.

....but mostly, a vacation home is a place to relax.

Bob and Eleanor saw their cabin as a place to rest, not work. Work was exactly what they were trying to get away from by going to the cabin. Of course, they recognized that owning a cabin necessarily involves a number of tasks. Bob and Eleanor studied those tasks, and then they devised simple systems that minimized the actual work required to keep the place going. When a problem arose that Bob was unable to tackle, he paid a local handyman to deal with it.

All of this is to suggest that there is a continuum of attitudes about maintaining recreational property. At one extreme end is my friend Bob, who owned a cabin for three decades without doing one thing to it that he didn't absolutely have to do. At the other extreme is John, who would rather work at his vacation home than relax in it.

Of course, there are many intermediate positions between the extremes represented by John and Bob. That middle ground is where most owners of vacation property find themselves. Most owners of recreational property do maintenance projects as the need arises, and they often enjoy a certain amount of puttering around, but they also try to make good use of their recreational property to rest their bodies and restore their spirits with relaxation.

THE PLAYHOUSE EFFECT

Owning a cabin has presented me with many surprises, but none was as unexpected as the discovery that work on the cabin doesn't feel like work.

While this isn't true for everyone, many people make the same discovery. Spending a weekend at home replacing a toilet usually feels like some form of punishment, and yet spending a weekend adding a deck to a vacation home usually feels like fun. Even people who abhor home maintenance often find that these projects feel different. A vacation home is a dollhouse, a place to play. Any work you do there is, by definition, fun.

This is hard to explain, and I probably shouldn't try to analyze this too much. It is more fun to do projects when you are working in a beautiful environment, for one thing. Second homes are often smaller than primary residences, so the projects have a limited scale, which is reassuring. But basically, I think the real difference between home maintenance and vacation home maintenance is mental. You fix the toilet at home so your kids can do Number Two, flush and not have everything end up on the bathroom floor. You build a woodshed because you have fantasies of spending happy weekends, ducking out to grab some dry firewood from your perfect woodshed. At bottom, things you have to do are work and things you do for fun are fun.

It doesn't work that way for everyone. Some people sell vacation property because they hate the responsibility of fixing things up on weekends. Others, like my friend Bob, make a study of minimizing the amount of time they "waste" doing maintenance on their recreational property. But if you are a new owner of recreational property, don't be surprised if you come to think of this as your playhouse and the time you spend improving or maintaining it feels more like fun than work.

WHAT KIND OF OWNER ARE YOU?

If you are new to this game, take some time to consider all the maintenance issues that will inevitably come up. How much fun are you likely to have working on your place? What sort of approach will you want to take to the maintenance of your recreational property? How will you use your recreational property? The answer has implications for what sort of maintenance program makes sense for you.

Your attitude might be affected by your job. If you are lucky enough to have a job that feels like fun, you probably won't mind spending a certain amount of your free time improving your vacation property. On the other hand, if you have a high stress job, you may want to relax during your time away. If the phone at the office rings all the time with new demands and you routinely bring work home because you can't keep up, you may not want the vexation of a long list of projects to finish on weekends.

There is the matter of the "busman's holiday." By tradition, the man who spends his week driving a bus might do many things on a weekend, but driving to some distant destination isn't likely to be one of them. Anyone who works with his or her hands all week long may dread fixing things during their free time. On the other hand, the accountant

Your vacation is the perfect place to pursue old hobbies, or develop new ones.

who sits in front of a computer all week might get a kick out of projects that involve sweat and tools and a bit of lifting. Change is bracing. Variety is fun.

Quite a few people are buying recreational property now as an investment. For them, working all weekend to improve the place might feel good because it increases the value of their investment.

People who buy property to serve as a base for sailing, fishing or hunting are going to have a very different perspectives. These people usually want to spend the maximum amount of time actively engaged in their favorite hobby. Time spent caulking windows is time lost from fishing. Families with young children might feel the same way—time spent with your kids when they are young is precious. Empty-nesters might get a kick out of working to make their hideaway more charming or convenient, but younger couples may not want maintenance projects to get in the way of sharing the joys of playing with their kids.

Ultimately, there is no single "right" or "normal" attitude toward the inevitable list of chores associated with home ownership. Owners who enjoy working with their hands and see their rural cottages as playhouses will have a ball improving that second home until, perhaps, the time comes to sell it and reap the benefits of all their labor. Others will want to study ways to minimize time "wasted" doing maintenance on their special place.

THE TWO PRIMARY LESSONS OF HOME MAINTENANCE

Sooner or later, homeowners learn a few bitter lessons. It is too bad, in a way, that schools don't teach classes in home maintenance. There is a great deal to know about keeping all of a home's essential systems functioning happily. This is no less true of vacation homes than of primary homes. In fact, in view of the fact you only get to be present at a vacation home for limited amounts of time, intelligent preventive maintenance may be even more important with your playhouse

than with your primary residence.

The first lesson most homeowners learn is that problems almost never solve themselves. Leaking faucets almost never seal themselves. Fans with burned out motors almost never rise from the dead and begin functioning again. Above all, most homeowners learn that problems involving water damage—such as a bad roof or improper weather sealing around windows—not only do not solve themselves, without attention they get worse. And worse.

Some minimal level of maintenance is unavoidable, and the sooner you attend to a problem, the better. The longer you delay dealing with a maintenance issue, the more serious the damage becomes and the more costly it is to repair. Millions of homeowners have discovered the truth of this observation the hard way. Home maintenance, like dental hygiene, is not optional. If you ignore your teeth, they go away. If you ignore vacation home maintenance, your home succumbs to the processes of decay and your property might defy trends by declining in value.

The second big truth is slightly more subtle, and many homeowners never quite get the point. The simple fact is that preventing a problem takes less time and costs less than solving it. The analogy in automobiles would be routine maintenance such as topping up the radiator with antifreeze and changing the oil. If you neglect those routine measures, you will have to deal with expensive problems some day. Many of us remember the television ads for oil filters that offered the choice of "Pay me now or pay me later."

And so it is with home maintenance, including the upkeep needed on cottages or other types of vacation homes. The problems you avoid by thinking and acting ahead are kinder on your checkbook and easier on your sweet disposition than the problems you ignore until you face an emergency. Doing things the quick, easy way usually turns out to be expensive and difficult.

Two basic facts apply to all types of recreational property owners.

First, if you own a second home or vacation property, a certain amount of maintenance is unavoidable. Things happen. Systems break down. The forces of sun, wind and rain are involved in a dark conspiracy to reduce every building to a pile of rubble. These forces must be thwarted with appropriate maintenance.

Second, the most efficient and effective maintenance program is one that you think through and plan carefully. If you handle every maintenance event on an ad hoc basis, you are doing a poor job of maintenance and a poorer job of using your precious time. Systematic, informed and anticipatory maintenance beats the heck out of panicky, sporadic disaster control after things have already gone bad.

It's a simple lesson. If you learn it by reading this book, you will get a wonderful return on your modest investment in the book. This book has been designed to help you enjoy your vacation home by using your precious time in ways that are efficient and effective. You want to keep your place in

HOME REPAIR IS IMPORTANT

Routine repair need not be an onorous chore—many people find maintaining a vacation home to be half the fun. If you focus on one thing, watch for places water can enter your home. An hour or two of caulking and sealing can be the best vacation home insurance you can buy.

good shape, even if you want to maximize your fun time and minimize the time you spend keeping it up. Smart maintenance ends up reducing the amount of time you waste doing miserable salvation projects and gives you more hours to truly enjoy your vacation home.

CHAPTER 2

VACATION HOMES AND WHAT MAKES THEM DIFFERENT

W HAT MAKES MAINTAINING A VACATION HOME ANY DIFFERENT FROM A PRIMARY HOME? AREN'T ALL HOMES MORE OR LESS THE SAME? AFTER ALL, EVERY HOME, NO MATTER WHETHER IT IS A VACATION OR A PRIMARY HOME, HAS A FOUNDATION, SOME INTERNAL AND EXTERNAL WALLS, AND A ROOF.

All homes have systems for controlling the temperature and systems for handling water. A tripped circuit breaker at a home in town is just like a tripped circuit breaker at a home on a lake or in the mountains. So what makes the maintenance of vacation homes any different from maintaining your primary residence?

Quite a few things, actually.

ISOLATION

Vacation homes usually are isolated. That is perhaps less true than it once was because new buyers are snapping up parcels of land that were considered undesirable just a few years ago. Vacant lots are being filled in. Beachfront recreational property is often densely developed. Still, compared to cities or even suburbs, most vacation property is located in thinly settled areas. Lucky cottage owners can't see the homes of adjacent properties.

Remoteness can be appealing. Remoteness, indeed, is one of the most important reasons people buy vacation homes. But remoteness has consequences, not all of which are positive.

Because cabins are usually tucked away in forests or on mountain-

Whether located on a seashore or deep in a mountain forest, many vacation homes are united by the fact that they are exposed to weather extremes and may be left unattended for long periods.

sides, vacation property owners have few neighbors. People who might be considered neighbors are likely to live farther away than the neighbors in a city or town. Even in recreational areas with relatively dense development, such as some stretches of seashore, you might not have neighbors close at hand because the people who would ordinarily be considered your neighbors might occupy the adjacent properties only at certain times of the summer. They just aren't around much. Being isolated is great when you want to quietly enjoy a sunset, and yet there are many times when it is useful to have friendly people living close by.

If your vacation property is isolated, lumberyards and hardware stores probably won't be close. Inexperienced people frequently make three or four trips to the hardware store to buy tools and supplies as they thrash through a simple repair. If the closest hardware store is 30 miles away, a project that should take an hour can easily fill a weekend.

Then, too, when the small-town hardware and lumber stores in vacation country typically have a meager selection of products, the prices tend to be higher than what you would pay in a "big box" style of home maintenance store.

PRIMITIVE SYSTEMS

The basic systems of many vacation homes are less sophisticated than those of modern homes. Remote recreational homes don't have sewer lines reaching them, so those

A gas-powered generator is a good idea in places where electrical utility service is unpredictable. In a remote cabin, generators can even serve as the sole source of electricity.

properties are likely to feature an outhouse, septic system or a composting toilet. A cabin high in the mountains or a cottage on an island might have no electricity, or may be powered by the limited output of a generator.

The primitive systems of recreational homes are both an advantage and a disadvantage. If your place doesn't have a toilet, you will never have to deal with a clogged toilet. If your secret cottage in the mountains lacks electricity, the soft light of oil lanterns will provide reliable illumination even if a windstorm drops trees on the local electric utility lines. Simple systems break down less frequently than complex systems.

The primary disadvantage of the simple technologies of many vacation homes is that you, the cabin owner, are often faced with maintenance issues at your cabin that you

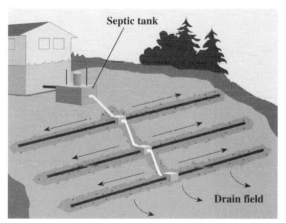

Private septic systems consist of an underground tank and a system of pipes fanning out from the tank. When sewage reaches the tank, the solid wastes settle to the bottom, where they are consumed by microorganisms. As the tank fills, the water flows out of the tank through porous drain pipes that distribute the water into the soil. The water is filtered clean as it drains down through thick layers of soil and rock on its return to the water table. Used correctly, a septic system requires only that residual solid wastes be pumped out every few years.

don't understand well. Septic system drain fields can develop problems you never encountered with your municipal sewer system. Heating a house with a wood stove might seem liberating, and yet there is a great deal to know about maintaining stoves safely. If you've always lived in homes with forced air heat and gas fireplaces, you may not know what rural people know about the virtues of dry firewood and prudent chimney maintenance. The maintenance issues you face at a home in the country are likely to be novel.

AMATEUR CONSTRUCTION

In any city, some homes are beautifully built by skillful carpenters and some are sloppily built. Older homes—those erected before building codes were put in place—are most likely to vary in quality. Even so, the range of soundness in city homes is not huge. Even old homes in cities have often been upgraded and brought up to code over the decades as they have been sold to new buyers.

This may be less true of vacation homes. Most vacation homes have been built in regions where anybody could put up any kind of structure, and whether the building was sound or wobbly was nobody else's business. Building codes regulating how close a house can be to the water are common, as are codes applying to septic systems. Beyond that, "anything goes" in many areas. If you want to build a home in the woods that violates every principle of sound construction, it is your money and your choice.

A man once built a cabin close to my cabin on Lake Superior. His site had a moderate slope, tipping toward the lake. This is a region where a few inches of topsoil and duff cover a solid base of sandstone. This man didn't want to bother drilling into that rock to pour concrete pillars for the foundation. That seemed like a lot of unnecessary work to him, so he built his cabin on pillars that terminated in large pads that rested directly on the ground. The structure wasn't anchored in any way, but that didn't strike this fellow as a problem. After all, where would an entire cabin go?

The answer turned out to be "into Lake Superior." Following the melt of snow and the rainstorms each spring, this man's cabin slid a few more feet down the hill toward the lake. This seemed funny at first. My neighbor claimed he had built his cabin a legal distance from the lake and it wasn't his fault that the shoreline and the view got closer each year. Eventually, this amateur cabin builder realized that his cabin would continue to slide down the hill until it ultimately tum-

Rural vacation homes are often informal in construction. This cabin was sided with short pieces of scrap cedar siding. Such homes require a bit more diligence when it comes to maintenance.

bled into the lake. Before that could happen, he set fire to his cabin and then hired a competent local craftsman to build a replacement.

This is an extreme example, but it is meant to make the point that buyers of recreational property have fewer safeguards than buyers of homes in cities and towns. In some areas, any fool with a hammer and a saw has the right to try to build a house, and so it is hardly surprising that the range of soundness in construction is frighteningly broad.

Another characteristic of vacation homes is that people sometimes build the smallest, least-expensive structure possible and later decide to increase functionality and living space by adding other units. They start with a small house, and then decide a garage with a workshop would be nice. Or they might build a screened porch and a sauna. Perhaps they try to tack on a big elevated deck. There is nothing wrong with adding buildings or extending the original structure, but these things are often done with little planning and not enough professionalism to make sure they are sound. The additions often have a "jerry-built" character that makes it necessary for later owners to do a lot of maintenance just to keep them in good shape.

WEATHER ISSUES

Vacation homes located in beautiful, remote areas are typically exposed to weather that is more destructive than the weather that prevails in major metro areas. My own cabin is an example. Located on the shores of Lake Superior, it shares the unique weather of the world's largest lake. Although my

Ice dams caused by melting snow have been known to cause severe damage to a structure.

primary home is only 220 miles from my cabin, the cabin has to withstand entirely different weather than my home. The snow is typically much deeper near the lake. The storms that lash its shores are more ferocious than anything my city home has to handle.

Usually, the fact that a vacation home is exposed to more violent weather is just a nuisance. Deep snowstorms can make it difficult to make it up the driveway, for example. Most recreational property owners simply adjust their schedules and use the property at times of year when weather isn't a problem.

Some weather-based problems, however, are more troublesome. What city-bred homeowners often fail to understand is that the extreme weather of many vacation areas has consequences for home maintenance. City folks with property along ocean beaches are surprised to learn that salt water, even the spray from salt water, creates maintenance issues. In northern regions, vacation homes may not be heated unless being used, and unheated cabins get extremely cold inside in winter. That can cause trouble in ways that will catch many cottage owners by surprise.

INFREQUENT RESIDENCE

Many recreational homes sit empty for several months at a stretch. While owners are away, maintenance problems crop up unseen and often continue to get worse until the owners finally return. New owners of cabins blithely assume they'll find the place in the same shape when they return as when they departed. They rarely do.

Some examples might illustrate this point. Perhaps your cottage has wooden steps leading to the front door, old wooden steps that became water-soaked until they have rotted and become weak between visits. Or, a small roof leak that you didn't notice on your last visit may have become larger while you were away. Or perhaps carpenter ants started snacking on the framework while you were away. Every week the house stood unoccupied, that colony of ants continued to gnaw away, turning critical structural supports into sawdust.

Infrequent use of vacation homes raises another issue, namely security. This isn't, strictly speaking, a "maintenance issue." But

Severe termite damage can be identified by channels cut into the wood by feeding insects.

BUILDING WOODEN PORCH STEPS

Wooden porch steps are easier to build than concrete steps, and they are less expensive. In addition, with paint and a complementary railing design, they can be built to match the style of your porch.

Wooden steps consist of three basic parts: stringers, treads, and risers. Stringers provide the framework and support for the steps, and are usually made from 2 × 12s. Treads are the stepping surfaces of the steps, and are usually made from 2 × 12s or pairs of 2 × 6s. Risers are the vertical boards at the back of each step, and are usually 2 × 6s or 2 × 8s.

If you are building replacement steps, use the dimensions of your old steps as a guide. If you are building new steps, you will have to create a plan, which will take a little bit of math and a little bit of trial and error.

When designing new steps, consider step dimensions, as well as style issues. However, before finalizing your plan, always check local code requirements. For example, codes may require a step railing when there will be two or more steps. In general, porch steps should be at least 3 ft. wide. To inhibit warping and provide better support, use three stringers, rather than two.

Wood steps do not require footings. Simply attach them to the rim joist or apron of the porch, and anchor them to the sidewalk at the base of the first step.

HOW TO MEASURE RISE & RUN

Step A: Measure the Run

1. Attach a mason's string to the porch rim joist, at the porch floor height, then drive a stake where you want the base of the bottom step to fall—plan for between 10" and 12" for each planned step. Attach the other end of the string to the stake and use a line level to level it.

2. Measure the length of the string—this distance is the overall depth, or run, of the steps. If necessary, you can increase the overall run by moving the stake at the planned base of the steps away from the house.

NOTE: If your steps contain a landing, attach the mason's string to the house foundation, 1" below the threshold of the door. Also, include the measurement of the landing (the width of the door plus 12") into the run dimension when planting the stake.

Step B: Measure the Rise

1. Measure down from the string to the bottom of the stake to determine the overall height, or rise, of the steps.

2. Divide the overall rise by the estimated number of steps. The rise of each step should be between 6" and 8". For example, if the overall rise is 21" and you plan to build three steps, the rise of each step would be 7" (21 divided by 3"), which falls within the recommended safety range for riser height.

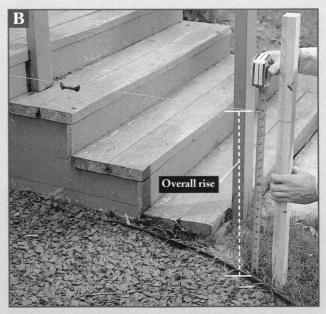

A Drive a stake where the base of the bottom step will be, then attach a level mason's string at the porch floor height and to the stake. Measure the distance from the house to the string for the overall run.

B Measure from the ground to the mason's string for the overall rise. Divide by the estimated number of steps to determine the riser height for each step. Riser heights should be uniform for each step, between 6" and 8".

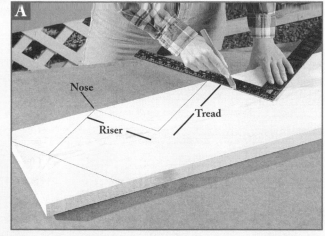

Following your step plan drawing, use a framing square to mark the layout on a step stringer. Mark the riser and tread sizes on each leg of the square, and make sure each "nose" falls on the same edge of the stringer.

HOW TO BUILD PORCH STEPS

Step A: Cut the Stair Stringers

1. Determine the rise and run for the steps (opposite page).

2. Sketch a detailed plan for the steps based on the rise and run dimensions. Use the dimensions to find the uniform height for the risers (6" to 8"), and the tread depth (10" to 12"). Adjust the parts of the steps as needed, staying within the given dimension ranges. Take time to create the final plan drawing; it is worth doing carefully.

3. Use a framing square to mark the step layout on a stringer—usually a 2 × 12—with the rise distance (riser) and run distance (tread) each noted on a leg of the square. Lay out the stringer so the "nose" areas where the tread and riser meet on each step fall at the same edge of the board. Check all angles with the square to make sure they are right angles.

4. Notch-out the stringer, using a circular saw for straight cuts, and finish the cuts with a handsaw where cuts meet at the inside corners. Use this stringer as a template for laying out and cutting two more stringers.

5. Mark and trim off the thickness of one tread (1$\frac{1}{2}$") at the bottom of each stringer so the rise of the bottom step will equal the rise of the other steps.

Step B: Attach the Stair Stringers

1. Attach evenly spaced metal angle brackets to the porch rim joist or apron, using 10d joist hanger nails. Make sure the brackets are perpendicular to the ground.

2. Position the stringers inside the angle brackets so the top of each stringer is 1$\frac{1}{2}$" below the top of the porch floor. Attach the stringers to the angle brackets with joist hanger nails.

Step C: Install the Gussets

1. Measure the distance between the stringer tops, then use these measurements to cut 2 × 4 gussets to length.

2. Make sure the stringers are square to the rim joist,

Evenly space three angled brackets on the rim joist, and fasten with 10d joist hanger nails.

Cut 2 × 4 gussets to size, position between the step stringers, and drill holes into the concrete with a masonry bit. Fasten the gussets to the concrete with 3" masonry screws.

Tools & Materials

- Tape measure
- Mason's line
- Line level
- Framing square
- Circular saw
- Handsaw
- Drill
- Level
- Clamps
- Wrench
- Jig saw
- Framing lumber
- Finish lumber
- Milled cap rail
- Metal corner brackets (3)
- 10d joist hanger nails
- 3" masonry screws
- $\frac{3}{8}$ × 6" carriage bolts with washers
- 2$\frac{1}{2}$" deck screws
- 3" deck screws
- 8d galvanized finish nails
- 8d galvanized casing nails

then position the gussets between the bases of the stringers. Drill holes through the gussets and into the concrete, $1/4"$ deeper than the embedment length of the screw. NOTE: Use a masonry bit recommended by the manufacturer of the masonry screws you choose. Oversized holes will make it difficult to set the masonry screws.

3. Clean out the holes, then fasten the gussets to the concrete with 3" masonry screws.

Step D: Attach the Railing Posts

1. Cut the 4×4 posts for the step railing to height. Position the posts at the outside face of an outside stringer. Make sure the posts are plumb, using a level, then clamp them in position. Drill $3/8"$ guide holes through the posts and the stringer.

2. Drive $3/8 \times 6"$ carriage bolts through the guide holes and secure each with a washer and nut on the inside face of the stringer.

Step E: Install the Step Risers & Treads

1. Measure the stringers for the dimensions of the risers. Cut to size, then attach the risers to the vertical edges of the stringers, using $2^{1}/2"$ deck screws.

2. Measure the depth of the step treads, adding 1" to 2" to both the depth and the length to create an over-hang. Cut to size, using a circular saw. Notch the treads for the top and bottom steps to fit around the posts, using a jig saw.

3. Position the treads, then attach to the horizontal edges of the stringers, using $2^{1}/2"$ deck screws.

Step F: Install the Bottom & Top Rails

1. Lay a 2×4 on the steps flush against the posts, then mark a cutting line on the 2×4 where it meets at each inside post edge. Use the 2×4 as a template for marking cutting lines on the top and cap rails.

2. Set the blade of a circular saw to match the angle of the cutting marks on the 2×4, then gang the 2×4 with a 2×2 for the top railing and a piece of cap railing for cutting. Gang-cut the rails at the cutting lines.

3. Toenail the bottom rail to the posts, using 3" deck screws driven through pilot holes and into the inside faces of the posts. The bottom of the rail should be level with the noses of the steps.

4. Attach the 2×2 top rail so it is parallel to the bottom rail, 2" down from the finished post height.

Step G: Install the Balusters & Top Cap

1. Hold a 2×2 flush against a post, so the ends extend past the top and bottom rails. Mark cutting lines on the 2×2 at the bottom edge of the top rail, and the top edge

Clamp railing posts into position, making sure they are plumb. Drill $3/8"$ holes through the posts and stringer, then secure with $3/8 \times 6"$ carriage bolts with washers.

Measure the dimensions for the risers and treads (adding 1" to 2" to treads for an overhang), and cut to size. Notch the treads to fit around posts as necessary. Attach with $2^{1}/2"$ deck screws.

of the bottom rail. Use the 2 × 2 as a template for making cutting lines on all railing balusters.

2. Mark layout lines for the balusters on the top and bottom rails, spacing the balusters no more than 4" apart.

3. Drill $1/8$" holes in the center of the top rail at baluster locations, then drive $2^1/2$" deck screws into the baluster ends. Toenail balusters to the bottom rail with 8d finish nails.

4. Cut the cap rail to size, then position over the top rail. Fasten with $2^1/2$" deck screws.

5. Install a bottom rail, top rail, and cap rail in a horizontal position between the railing post at the top step and the end post for the porch railing. If the distance between posts is more than 4", install balusters between the rails.

Step H: Close off Gaps & Finish the Steps

1. Attach nailing strips to the undersides of the outer stringer, set back far enough to create a recess for the wood or lattice.

2. Cut a piece of wood or lattice to fit, and install it with 8d casing nails.

3. Check the post tops with a straightedge to make sure they follow the slope of the railing. Trim to height, if necessary, then attach decorative post caps, if desired.

4. Apply sealer/protectant or paint the steps and railing to match the porch and house.

Cut a 2 × 4 bottom rail to size, position between the posts, and toenail in place with 3" deck screws. Install the 2 × 2 top rail similarly, but centered on the posts.

Measure along the top rail and mark the baluster locations so they are no more than 4" apart. Drill pilot holes through the top rail for fastening the balusters.

Install nailing strips behind the stringers. Measure and cut finished lumber to size to close off the gap, and fasten in place with 8d casing nails.

it is close enough. Keeping your cabin safe from human intruders is similar to keeping it safe against weather and furry intruders.

CRITTERS

Vacation homes are, almost by definition, sited in areas that naturally are home to higher populations of wild critters than are found in suburbs or central cities. Seeing wildlife is one of the main reasons people love recreational homes, but it is no joy to view wildlife in your home. A major difference between primary residences and vacation homes is that wild critters create maintenance problems that city-dwelling folks don't anticipate and don't usually know how to handle.

The animals that threaten vacation homes run the gamut of size and type. Cluster flies are destructive and messy. Bats, looking for a cave to huddle in, fly down chimneys. High mosquito populations can virtually make you a prisoner indoors, unable to do anything outside. Porcupines girdle and kill trees. Skunks build dens under sheds and start making more skunks. Raccoons break into attics to set up housekeeping, and one of the most humbling experiences available to a homeowner is trying to outwit raccoons. Finally, no animal on the continent can equal the ability of the black bear to trash a house. All across the country, rising bear populations are forcing people to change the way they use their vacation homes.

If any animal is more of a headache for owners of recreational property than those already mentioned, it is the mouse. Mice are incredibly enterprising when it comes to finding cracks in foundations. Mice seem

cute and are fun to watch until they demonstrate their destructive potential.

Animals are wonderful when they live where they were meant to live. Animals that come indoors to live can do an astonishing amount of damage. One of the harsh lessons of rural life is that you often have to go to war to protect your property against critters. This creates maintenance challenges that are new and complicated for people whose city experiences have not taught them how deal with the critters.

GROUNDS KEEPING

Vacation home owners are often jolted by the difficult array of tasks related to keeping their grounds or lawn in good order. First, there is simply a lot of work to be done. No matter what your vacation property looks like, maintaining it can require a great deal of work. The work is minimized if you intend to keep your grounds in a natural condition. If you mean to whip nature into shape and keep your vacation property as neat as a suburban lot, your work will be never-ending.

This area of maintenance is complicated and messier than most owners expect. Trees are always blowing down or losing limbs. Weeds and shrubs continually grow and alter the look of the area. Many owners are shocked by how frequently they lose trees to storms. When these people plant young trees to replace ones they have lost, a second shock is how young trees can be killed by ravenous deer or extreme heat or cold.

Unfortunately, the only background most

owners bring to the challenges of maintain ing the grounds of their vacation property is the experience of tending a suburban or city lawn. When they attempt to subject wilder lands to the same standards of uniform neatness, they alter the character of the land and commit themselves to virtually endless toil. Sometimes what seem like simple efforts to trim back a bit of brush can end up with cascading unintended consequences.

There are wiser alternatives, as we will see. For now it is only important to note that maintaining a city lawn and maintaining vacation property are not the same thing at all.

COMMUNITY RELATIONS

For many new owners of recreational property, the biggest surprise is learning that their purchase has made them a new figure of consequence in a pre-existing community. Even in undeveloped areas, there will be people living in the general area of your vacation property. Those people might have feelings about new owners.

Most purchases cause the new owners to join—if only superficially—the community of the nearest town. Too often, they fail to think about what their presence can mean to people who live in that community all of the time. They have a home elsewhere, so the new owner fails to understand that they might be a significant new presence in the sparsely populated area where they just purchased their hideaway.

This can be a happy or an unhappy discovery. Much depends on the specific cir-

CREATURE OF THE NIGHT

A friend once used our cabin early in the spring. When he returned from his weekend, I asked how it had gone.

"Oh, great! I had terrific cross-country skiing. The cabin came through the winter in good shape. But, uh, there was one thing."

"What was that?"

"You've got some kind of animal living in your cabin."

"Animal?"

"Yeah. It was kinda spooky. I never saw such a thing before."

"Well, what was it?"

"I don't know! I was sitting in the living room while the stove warmed the place up when I saw this face looking at me from behind a curtain. Scared me! So I went and got a broom. When I got close to this thing, it amazed me by sailing clear across the room. I kept coming after it, and it kept zooming through the air. After a while, I decided I never was going to get it, so I got smart. I cranked a window open, and sometime in the night it left."

"So it's gone?"

"I think. Do you know if flying squirrels live in Wisconsin?"

cumstances, but much also depends on the attitudes of the new owners of remote lands. If they are insensitive to the perspectives of people who live in that area all year long, they can inflame resentment. If they are thoughtful and respectful in their dealings with local people, those local people can contribute immeasurably to making vacation home ownership a joyful experience.

CHAPTER 3

DIFFERENT TYPES OF VACATION HOMES

VACATION HOMES COME IN ALL SIZES AND SHAPES. THERE ARE A-FRAMES, RUSTIC LOG CABINS, GEODESIC DOMES, CONVENTIONAL FRAMED STRUCTURES, AND HOUSES IN SHAPES THAT DON'T HAVE A NAME. MY OWN CABIN MIGHT BE BEST DESCRIBED AS A "SEXTA-DECIMAL QUAKER OATS VERNACULAR." THAT IS, MY CABIN IS A SIXTEEN-SIDED THING THAT RESEMBLES AN OATMEAL BOX. THERE IS ONLY ONE LIKE IT, WHICH MIGHT BE A GOOD THING. The man who designed and built my cabin described it as "a bad design, poorly executed." One cabin I know in northern Wisconsin is a converted fishing trawler that somehow manages to look like a 1930s diner. In short, there is no limit to the different forms a vacation home can take.

In terms of maintenance, things are simpler. We can divide the world of vacation homes in several simple ways. From the perspective of maintenance, these houses are old or they are new; they were built soundly or they were slapped together; they are large or they are small; they are complex or they are simple. That is what counts.

OLD OR NEW

Vacation homes can be old, new or middle-aged. Some experts consider any home over 40 years old an "old" structure. Construction techniques and home building technology were different half a century ago. Of course, some very old cabins were lovingly crafted by skilled workmen of a sort that doesn't exist these days, but they are rare. A great many old vacation homes are hard to maintain just because they are old.

There are several maintenance consequences if you own an old vacation home. For one thing, older houses need more tender loving care. Roofs need to be restored from time to time. Foundations crumble during late winter freeze-thaw cycles. Well pumps give out. Foundations are more likely to have multiple cracks in subtle places that you can't find, but that legions of mice can find.

Older houses also are more of a pain to work on. If you go to a small-town hardware store to find a replacement plumbing fixture, you might find that your cabin's plumbing is so old its components are out of style and not stocked. Older structures were sometimes built with poor access to critical areas when you need to do maintenance. Sometimes old cabins were built without any notion that plumbing or electricity would be added to them, and the ad hoc way these systems are sometimes added can increase your maintenance challenges.

SOUNDNESS

As we noted in the discussion of all the ways vacation homes can differ from primary homes, many cabins are designed and erected by amateurs. This book is not a guide to buying vacation homes, but one of the first questions any prospective buyer should ask is "who built this thing, and did they know what the heck they were doing?"

If you are in a position to purchase a home built by someone who wasn't sure which end of the hammer to hold, you still might want to do it. Amateurs sometimes rise above themselves. But if you become the owner of a building erected by someone who marched to a different drummer and let intuition or a tight budget dictate the structure and design of the home, maintenance issues can dominate your experience.

Creativity is a wonderful thing, but not when it comes to the fundamentals of home construction. There are just a few sound ways to frame a structure and many inventive ways that can lead to trouble. For windows to open easily and close in a weather-tight way, they have to be installed "just so." There's nothing wrong with designing a vacation home in the shape of a doughnut if that is what your dreams require, but there is a great deal wrong with any home whose roof doesn't ventilate moisture while retaining heat.

Vacation homes designed and built by amateurs are usually more affordable than those erected by professional carpenters. Recreational property prices have gotten so high that many would-be owners are forced to buy properties that were more whacked together than designed. If your place is like that, you can still have wonderful times there, but you better have an idea of what you're getting into. The less competently built the house is, the more you will have to do in the way of maintenance.

LARGE OR SMALL

Vacation homes come in all sizes, although at some point you simply have to say that a "cabin" with three stories, a deck, a patio, six bedrooms, a media room and a swimming pool is just a city home situated in the woods.

Large homes are more difficult to keep up than small ones. Each window is another place where weather stripping can fail and water might seep in. The larger the volume of the house, the more difficult it will be to keep warm or cool. The initial cleanup of a cozy

One small, old, rustic and remote; the other expansive, new, modern and quite cosmopolitan. Yet both are vacation homes. General maintenance isn't much different, but the scale of the work required may vary widely.

little cottage goes much faster than it possibly can for a big vacation home with many rooms.

Size, in this sense, is more than the physical dimensions. If you have outbuildings, they in effect increase the size of the structures you need to maintain. It is typical of vacation homes that they are built, and then years later other structures are added, and each additional building adds to the maintenance burden. For example, on my property I have two biffies, a woodshed and a gazebo. Each one of these outbuildings has a roof to keep up and walls which critters are always trying to chew their way through. As small as my cabin is, the maintenance issues are considerable because of all of those additional buildings.

The size of the property matters, too. If you have a zero-maintenance approach to the upkeep of your lands, it probably doesn't make much of a difference if you own half an acre or 80 acres of timbered land. But most vacation property owners end up doing much more work on their land than they ever expected: planting desirable plants, cutting up downed timber, removing unwanted brush, weeding the driveway and dealing with storm damage.

SIMPLE/COMPLEX

From the perspective of maintenance, perhaps the biggest difference between vacation homes is the relative complexity of their systems. Each additional major system adds maintenance needs. If a property has electricity, there are a few more things to maintain than if it's a remote mountain cabin with no electricity. A cabin with a pump is more complex to maintain than one where you fetch water from a nearby spring. Any home with a pool or hot tub has maintenance issues that don't exist for a simpler property.

The trend toward complexity is unmistakable. At one time, vacation homes were seen as escapes from the hectic pace of modern life. People built simple cabins, often later compromising by connecting them to electricity and perhaps installing a drain field septic system. But tastes have swung strongly toward vacation homes with the modern amenities. Many modern Americans cannot imagine a home—even a vacation home— without cable television reception, electricity to power a sound system, a telephone and some sort of Internet access.

WEATHERSTRIPPING DOUBLE-HUNG WINDOWS

In most climates, weatherstripping is essential to keep windows energy efficient. It prevents heat loss in the winter, heat gain in the summer, and also provides a barrier against moisture and insects.

Start by removing the double-hung window, and removing any old, worn-out weatherstripping. Clean the tracks thoroughly.

Cut metal V-channel weatherstripping to fit in the channels for the sliding sash **(photo A)**, extending at least 2" past the closed position for each sash (don't cover the sash-closing mechanism). Attach the V-channel by driving wire brads with a tack hammer. Drive the fasteners flush with the surface, so the sliding sashes won't catch on them.

Flare out the open end of the V-channels with a putty knife so the channel is slightly wider than the gap between the sash and the track it fits into **(photo B)**. Avoid flaring out too much at one time—it's difficult to press the V-channel back together without causing buckling.

Now, wipe down the underside of the bottom window with a damp rag and let it dry. Attach self-adhesive foam or rubber weatherstripping to the underside of the sash **(photo C)**.

Seal the gap between the top sash and the bottom sash. Lift the bottom sash and lower the top sash to improve access, then tack metal V-channel weatherstripping to the bottom rail on the top sash **(photo D)**. The open end of the V should be pointed down to prevent moisture from infiltrating the joint. Flare out the V-channel, using a putty knife.

Cut and attach metal V-channel weatherstripping to the side channels for the sliding sash. The open side of the V should face the outdoors.

Flare the V-channel open slightly, using a putty knife. This will improve the seal of the weatherstripping.

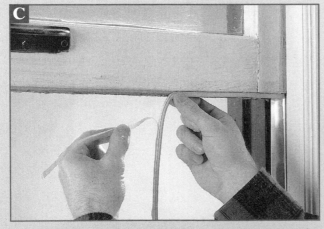

Apply self-adhesive foam or rubber weatherstripping to the underside of the sash.

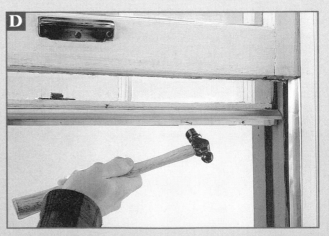

Apply V-channel weatherstripping to the bottom rail on the rear window.

Many vacation homes are located on waterfront property. Docks, which are common, are a lot of work. First, they usually require quite a bit of work to put in and take out. Obviously, some designs go in and come out much more readily than others. But because docks are in the water and usually get pushed around by wave action and the tugging of a tethered boat, they are subject to wear. Anything that is exposed to water is going to rot and break down sooner or later.

All mechanical systems are apt to require care from time to time, but the system most likely to be affected by weather and seasonal use is plumbing. Vacation home plumbing is much more likely to be troublesome than the plumbing in your primary home.

Tradeoffs

Let's say you are the type of person who gets a big kick out of fixing things up. Maintenance on your vacation home and its outbuildings is actually fun. From that perspective, you are going to be ecstatic if you have a large property with many outbuildings that are both old and amateurishly built. If you bought a place with a plumbing system, electricity, an Internet connection, telephone service and a dock, you don't have to worry about what to do with your spare time because fixing up your vacation property can be almost a full-time job!

A person who primarily wants to enjoy the area rather than "wasting time" on home maintenance is going to be happy with a small, simple and modern house on a modest amount of land. If the house was intelligently

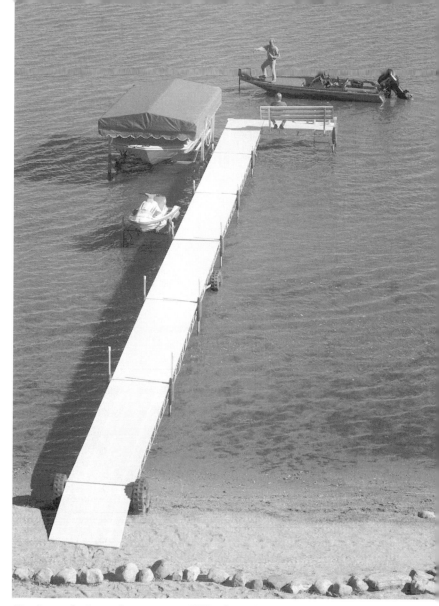

Having a dock need not create difficult maintenance chores. This light-weight dock, complete with sitting bench, can be rolled in and out of water at the beginning and end of your vacation season.

designed and built by real carpenters, maintenance issues will be trivial.

Many owners of recreational property fall somewhere in the middle. For many of us, the challenge of keeping up our vacation property comes down to using our maintenance time as intelligently as possible.

CHAPTER 4

OPENING WEEKEND

During the off-season, you dream about getting back to "Shangri La" or whatever your family calls your vacation home. While shoveling winter snow, you thought about the improvements you want to make to it. At odd moments at the office, you made ambitious plans for the garden you could put in.

Throughout those months of long nights, you grinned as you anticipated all the fun your family would have when you got back to your vacation home. Sometimes it seemed that Opening Weekend would never come. But then it did.

Opening Weekend is the time when you check out the house and prep it for the rest of the season. It usually involves quite a bit of work, but it is happy work.

Depending on where you live and how you use your vacation property, Opening Weekend might come at different times. Since many such homes are located in northern or mountainous regions, a great many are used lightly—if at all—during the winter. For many owners, Memorial Day is the semi-official opening. Memorial Day gives families a three-day weekend late in May. In view of the travel time required to get to there and back, having that extra day helps you clean and open the property while still allowing a little time for fun.

Similarly, many families use Labor Day weekend for shutting down the place for the season. Labor Day, the first Monday in September, yields another three-day weekend. It is a logical time to haul in the dock, mothball all implements with gasoline motors, shut off all the mechanical systems and button everything down.

Opening Weekend is much more fun. If you are far enough from neighbors, you can put a bouncy, upbeat disk in your CD player and crank up the volume. Many hands make for fast work. Come prepared with a definite plan for what you want to accomplish, but have fun.

HAVE A PLAN

Opening Weekend is an emotional moment, but it is also an important opportunity to get the season off to the right start. The Opening Weekend visit is the best time to assess the condition of the place and either do seasonal maintenance or plan projects that will set things right and make it possible to enjoy many carefree fun visits later.

When families first purchase vacation property, they naturally think mainly about the fun they can have there. It usually takes time and a few unhappy surprises for them to learn how much work it takes to keep a second home functioning well. That relates to the classic dilemma of the vacation property owner: how do you keep up with all the chores and still have enough time to have fun?

It can be done. The way that works best for most people is to make a routine of the important maintenance tasks. Any job takes longer if you have to think about it and collect the tools to do it. If you put it off you just add to the amount of time you lose on that task. Instead of putzing around with maintenance, savvy owners set up routines that allow them to fly through the necessary tasks.

Habit is a powerful tool. The first time you do a task you might not be terribly efficient. The next time you do it, you know which tools you need and what steps you need to take to perform the task. In time, your family will learn to divide up the little maintenance tasks among different family members. Make lists, plan ahead and be prepared with all the necessary tools and supplies. Even if you are chronically unprepared and disorganized in other areas of life, it is possible to create a set of habits and routines that make maintenance far less troublesome than it might be.

If it isn't too late to do so, consider contacting the former owners to ask what routines they had for opening and closing the place. The previous owners probably discovered that some routine maintenance was critically important and some seemingly useful steps were just a waste of time. Those folks probably acquired a to-do list that helped them whip things into shape each season.

You probably don't want to invite a guest along for the opening weekend (or any time when the place has been idle for a long period of time). If a guest is a really good sport, he or she might find splitting wood or installing the dock fun. Still, most families find that it works best to make opening weekend a special time when the family runs through the list of important start-up procedures. It often takes as long to teach a newcomer what to do as it takes to do the task with a fewer number of experienced family members.

WALK-AROUND

When you arrive, the first job is to assess the condition of things. Do a complete walk-around of the house and the grounds. You might want to carry a little tablet so you can jot down notes to follow up on later. Each property is unique and has unique

Mold not only looks (and usually smells) horrible, but it may well be consuming the wall and the framing behind it.

maintenance requirements, but here is a checklist of things you might want to inspect on your first visit of the season:

• Look for fallen trees and limbs, especially if they have struck any of your buildings. Decide what you will need to do to deal with downed trees or limbs—let them rot where they are, cut them up and leave them on the ground to decompose, cut them up and dispose of them somewhere or cut them up and stack them for use as firewood. Investigate whether or not you are losing trees to porcupines.

• Check the condition of the grounds. Are there any invasive species muscling their way in? Do you see any new trees, bushes or plants growing that you want to encourage or discourage?

• Turn on the electrical power (flipping all the circuit breakers or using the main lever at the power box). Check your major appliances to see if they are running. If you unplugged them when closing down, plug them back in now.

• Look for evidence of mice or nuisance insects. Do you see mouse poop or ripped up tissue paper where they have been making

nests? Any sign of chewing insects (like sawdust) or pupae? Any odd smells? If you covered the furniture when shutting down the cabin, gather up the covers. Check furniture upholstery for signs of mouse damage and mildew.

• Check out the house itself. Does it seem to be in good shape? Any roof leaks? Any signs of dry rot? Walk around outside, checking to see that the foundation seems sound. Did you lose any screens or windows to storms or critter attacks?

• Similarly, if you have outbuildings (shed, outhouse, gazebo, garage), check on their condition.

• Check how clean or dirty the place is. You might want to make notes on what cleanup will be required; especially if you see the need to clean something that usually doesn't require attention.

• If you have telephone service, make sure it is functional.

• If you have a pool or hot tub, check out its condition and mechanical systems.

If the system has breakers, turn each one off and back on. You should feel a firm click when you press the switch back to the on position. If the breaker doesn't click into place or the lever feels at all loose, consult an electrician.

Water system start-up

One critical Opening Weekend task is getting the water system functional. And as we often have to say, the exact procedures you need to follow will vary according to the exact nature of your water system.

My cabin represents one ridiculous extreme. My water system is a collection of colorful nylon jugs that hold about seven gallons of water apiece. My cabin has a "running water system" in the sense that I run to town with these jugs and fill them up from a pipe that spouts pure water from an artesian well. For me, getting my water system functional in spring amounts to filling the jugs.

Most water systems are more complex. If your system draws water from a well, you have a pump, and pumps differ. Some need to be primed each spring; most do not. Some have filters and some do not. Spring is the obvious time to install a new filter. Additional complexity is related to the number of fixtures in your plumbing system.

Your best course of action when purchasing a vacation home is to interview the owner at

After turning on the water, take a quick tour and inspect the pipes for leaks.

length about how he or she mothballed the water system at season's end and then restored it on Opening Weekend. Pay attention and take notes! If you didn't have the opportunity to ask these questions at the time of purchase, consider looking up the former owner now.

If you don't have the benefit of the previous owner's advice, consider hiring a local plumber to inspect your water system. Ask that plumber to describe a sensible program for shutting down the system and later turning the whole system back on.

The water system is of such great concern because of a curious characteristic of water. Water expands when it freezes. There is nothing about cold weather that is directly threatening to most vacation homes or their contents, but water can do great damage. The damage you need to fear most urgently is to elements of the water system: toilets, pipes, tanks, pumps and water heaters.

How you restore your water system to full functionality depends, of course, on how your system is configured and what steps you took to shut it down at the end of the previous system.

Here is how my uncle Don brings the water system of his northern Wisconsin cabin back to life:

• He attaches a hose to his pressure tank, and then turns on the power to the well pump. When the power comes on, fresh water enters the system and begins to move through all the pipes in the cabin, washing out any remaining old water and antifreeze.

• While that is in process, my uncle installs a new water filter.

WELL PUMPS

Well water systems use a pump to extract water from the underground aquifer, sending it up through the well pipe and storing it in a pressurized tank. There are two types of pumps used in most residential wells: the submersible pump and the jet pump.

Submersible pumps are popular today because they are more reliable for everyday use and require less maintenance than jet pumps. A submersible pump is a single unit that is submerged in the bottom of the well and uses a series of stacked impellers to drive water to the surface **(photo A)**. Submersible pump motors can operate trouble-free for more than 20 years. But repairing or replacing the pump requires a truck-mounted derrick.

Jet pumps are typically used with shallow wells or with wells used seasonally, such as at summer cabins. The jet pump mechanism combines the forces of a centrifugal pump and a jet nozzle to suck water up to the surface.

A single-drop jet pump is used for wells with a depth of up to 30 feet, at average elevations **(photo B)**. In deeper wells, where pressure must be greater to extract the same amount of water, a double-drop jet pump is used. This is similar to the single-drop pump but includes a surface impeller that directs a portion of the water back down the well. The water exits through an ejector at the bottom of the well, creating pressure to aid the pumping process.

As the pump draws the water from the well, it deposits it into a galvanized steel water tank, usually located in the basement of the house. As the tank fills, the air pressure inside the tank increases until it trips a pressure switch, which turns off the pump. The compressed air in the tank provides the pressure to supply the faucets. As water is drawn from the tank, the air pressure drops until the pressure gauge restarts the pump.

Standard storage tanks are subject to a problem called "waterlogging." This occurs when water in the tank absorbs the air, disrupting the balance between the water level and the pressurized air cushion. When the pressure system has little "give," slight changes in the water level cause the tank pressure to drop, and the pump turns on. This places stress on the pump, and should be corrected as soon as possible.

Some newer storage tanks have a rubber diaphragm that separates the water and air, preventing the absorption of the air into the water.

Another common problem with pump systems is low water pressure in the house supply system. Often, this can be corrected by adjusting the pressure gauge on the pump.

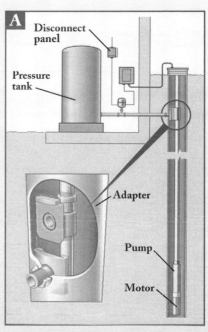

A submersible pump is a single unit that is submerged in the bottom of the well and uses a series of stacked impellers to drive water to the surface.

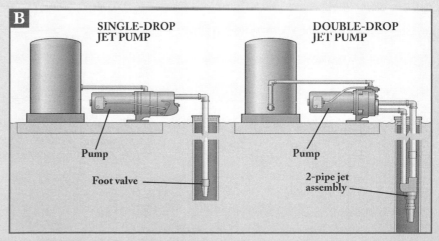

Jet pumps are located on the surface.

REGULAR MAINTENANCE SCHEDULE

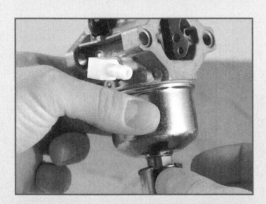

Y ou can avoid many small engine problems and save money on parts and repairs if you follow a regular maintenance schedule. Make good maintenance a habit when your engine is new, and always consult your owner's manual for special guidelines for your make and model. Service the engine more frequently if you use it heavily or under dusty or dirty conditions.

After the first five hours of use:
• Change the oil and filter.

After each use:
• Check the oil.
• Remove debris around the muffler.

Every 25 hours or every season:
• Change the oil if operating under heavy load or in hot weather.
• Service the air cleaner assembly.
• Clean the fuel tank and line.
• Clean the carburetor float bowl, if equipped.
• Inspect the rewind rope for wear.
• Clean the cooling fins on the engine block.
• Remove debris from the blower housing.
• Check engine compression.
• Inspect governor springs and linkages.
• Inspect ignition armature and wires.
• Inspect the muffler.
• Check the valve tappet clearances.
• Replace the spark plug.
• Adjust the carburetor.
• Check the engine mounting bolts/nuts.

Every 100 hours or every season:
• Clean the cooling system.*
• Change the oil filter, if equipped.
• Decarbonize the cylinder head.

Clean more often if the engine operates under dusty conditions or in tall, dry grass.

- He flips the circuit breaker so power is restored to the electric hot water heater.
- When the water has run for about 20 minutes, it will run clear and taste sweet. Uncle Don checks that. When the water quality is perfect again, he can turn off the pump and remove the hose.

He then turns off all faucets and spigots in the house—shutting them. (Part of the shut-down process in the fall is to leave all faucets open.) The water system is now good to go.

Other plumbing systems require different protocols. Some are designed so the old water is blown out with air pressure in spring. Some pumps need to be primed before they will function. You have to learn the right steps to bring your system back to life.

SMALL ENGINE MAINTENANCE

Most vacation home owners depend on a variety of devices powered by small gas engines. Many owners also have weed whips, brush cutters, all-terrain-vehicles, lawnmowers, snowmobiles, and outboard motors, firewood splitters or generators that are driven by gas engines.

The important care for all of these implements comes not when they're brought out for the season but when they're put away. The most important step is to protect the gas. Whenever gas is allowed to sit for several weeks, it begins to separate and form a varnish coating that coats the gas tank and clogs the carburetors. Hardware stores and many rural gas stations sell products that stabilize gas.

When opening the place for the season, your job is to refill the gas tanks and check the engines. Be careful to use the appropriate type of gas—pure gas for 4-cycle engines and gas/oil mix for 2-cycle engines.

Consider doing these routine maintenance procedures on your gas-powered tools on Opening Weekend:

- Replace dirty oil in four-stroke engines (engines that have a separate oil fill cap).
- Inspect oil filters, replacing those that are dirty or clogged.
- Inspect air filters, replacing or washing them as needed.
- Inspect spark plugs, replacing or re-gapping the plugs as needed.

Above all, as part of your Opening Weekend routine you should start up each gas-powered implement. If you can get your chain saw or outboard running now, it is sure to start when you need it during the season.

If you absolutely cannot get one of your gas-powered tools running during Opening Weekend, consider taking it to the nearest small engine repair specialist. These people are usually not hard to find in regions where many people own vacation property, and most of them charge less for tuning up a small engine than you would pay a lawnmower repair specialist in a metro area. Fix your engine yourself if you can, but don't be afraid to use the expertise of local repair experts.

Boat and motor maintenance is beyond the scope of this book, but it should go without saying that you want to service your boat and get the engine purring before you launch it for the first time. You can start an outboard motor in your garage or workshop if you clamp "ears" around the lower unit water intake

Servicing a foam air cleaner

1. Loosen the screws or wing nuts that hold the air cleaner assembly in place **(photo A)**. Disassemble.

2. Inspect the foam element. Replace it if it is torn or shows signs of considerable wear.

3. Saturate the new element with engine oil **(photo B)**. Then, squeeze it to spread the oil throughout. Wrap foam in clean cloth and squeeze to remove excess oil.

4. Inspect the rubbery sealing gasket between the air cleaner and carburetor. Replace it if it is worn.

5. Reassemble and reinstall the air cleaner.

Servicing a pleated-paper or dual-element air cleaner

Dual-element air cleaners come in a variety of designs. Two of the most common are shown here.

1. With the cover removed, separate the pre-cleaner (if equipped) from the cartridge **(photo C)**.

2. Tap the cartridge gently on a flat surface to remove any loose dirt. Inspect the element and replace it if it is heavily soiled, wet or crushed.

3. Inspect the pre-cleaner, if equipped. Note the mesh backing, designed to act as a barrier between the oily pre-cleaner and the pleated-paper element. Replace when soiled or worn or after 25 hours of use.

4. Look for oiling instructions on the pre-cleaner **(photo D)**. If directed, lubricate the pre-cleaner with oil. NOTE: Not all foam pre-cleaners should be oiled.

5. Clean the cartridge housing with a dry cloth **(photo E)**. Do not clean with solvents or compressed air.

6. Reassemble the air cleaner. If the pre-cleaner is the oiled type, take care to insert the mesh toward the paper element so that the paper is never exposed to the oil.

7. Reinstall, making sure that any tabs on the cartridge are in their slots on the engine housing. Gaps around the cartridge permit unfiltered air and damaging dirt particles to enter the engine.

PAPER FILTERS AND TIPPING THE ENGINE

If your engine has a paper filter cartridge, remove it temporarily any time you are preparing to tip the engine on its side. You'll eliminate any chance that oil from the pre-cleaner will spill onto the paper and ruin it. To prevent debris from entering the carburetor, temporarily cover the carburetor opening with plastic.

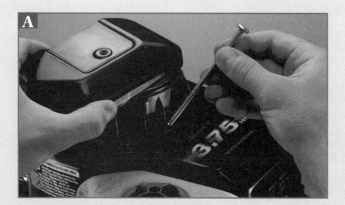

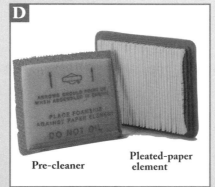

Pre-cleaner   Pleated-paper element

ports and run water through a hose to them. If your motor is going to be balky, you want to learn that in your workshop, not on the water with the boat full of expectant friends.

BATTERIES

There was a time when a vacation home could run without any batteries, but that time was many decades ago. Batteries now supply vital energy for all sorts of devices: cordless telephones, flashlights, lanterns, radios, CD players, MP3 players, DVD players, camcorders, cameras, boom boxes, clocks, weather stations, smoke alarms, alarm clocks and other gadgets.

To keep all of these devices performing well, you will need a collection of AAA, AA, D, C and 9-volt batteries. Many people find that alkaline batteries offer good performance at a reasonable price. Rechargeable batteries used to suffer from wimpy performance, giving out at awkward moments, but the Ni MH (Nickel Metal Hydride) battery has changed the way many people regard rechargeable batteries. Ni MH batteries are long-lived. Although initially expensive, they save you money in the long run because you can repeatedly recharge them. These batteries are attracting the attention of people who dislike discarding disposable batteries.

Take some time on Opening Weekend to test each flashlight and other battery-driven device. You can check the health of the batteries with an inexpensive battery tester (they sell for $8 to $12). Most owners bring a large supply of fresh batteries with them on Opening Weekend, bringing back the dead ones to be recycled properly.

A dock often serves the same role for a vacation home as the backyard deck does for a suburban residence. It's a place to relax and reflect, not just park the boat.

If you use 6- or 12-volt wet cell batteries, clean the corrosion off the terminals each spring. Auto and marine supply stores sell products (including wire brushes and anti-corrosion jellies) that can help you get clean terminals that make solid contact with the wire leads. Recharge the batteries with a high quality trickle charger. Re-install the batteries in their respective implements and make sure the connections are good and the battery took a good charge.

INSTALL THE DOCK

If you have waterfront property, it's generally ideal to put in your dock on Opening Weekend. Frankly, putting out the dock can be such a big job that you might not be able to do this on your first visit. After you do all the tasks needed to clean and check everything out, there might not be enough time on Opening Weekend to install a difficult dock. Much depends on the design and size of your dock. The job can be complicated by the

Cleaning should be among the first items on your to-do list after you arrive. It also provides a chance to inspect everything carefully.

kind of bottom that prevails along the shoreline. Mucky bottoms present one kind of difficulty. Steeply sloping bottoms are difficult in other ways.

If the lake frontage slopes sharply into deeper water, you only need a short dock, even if you will be mooring a large craft there. But if your property lies along a shallow bay, you might need to run a dock a long way to get it out where a boat can safely approach it.

Docks differ enormously in terms of how user-friendly they are. Some involve heavy, cumbersome frames, whereas others have frames that are light and easily adjusted. Most docks are designed to be put out in sections, with each section serving as a base for the next. Other docks have to be manhandled with great effort, with at least one person in waders in the water. In short, putting out a dock can be an orderly job or it can be a nightmare that involves Herculean effort and a lot of blue language.

The two most common types of docks are flotation docks and pipe docks. Flotation docks have decking mounted on some sort of flotation material, pods or cylinders. Pipe docks have wooden decks attached by brackets to metal frames. There are places where a dock can be left in place. In such cases, a permanent dock of cast concrete is always preferable to one that has to be taken out and put back in each season. Unfortunately, few places are appropriate for permanent docks.

Floating docks, which are highly versatile, are generally more appropriate for situations where docks are short and water levels fluctuate. If you are pushing a dock out into a marshy area with a soft bottom, think of a floating dock. Floating docks don't work where the water might drop to levels too shallow to hold up the floatation pods. It isn't safe to moor a heavy boat to a floating dock. The flotation material in some less expensive docks breaks down, crumbles and degrades the environment. The better (and more expensive) floatation docks don't break down this way.

Pipe docks are more suited to larger docks and those that extend out into deeper water. Heavier pipe docks can be difficult to put out just because of their weight, but they will hold a large boat more safely than a light pipe dock. Pipe docks can be adjusted as water levels fluctuate, although changing the height of a large pipe dock can be a tedious process. The environmental impact of a good pipe dock is minimal.

The whole issue of dock technology is complicated and worth serious study. One excellent reference is a book, *The Dock Manual,* by Max Burns. If the dock was in

Cleaning and inspecting a spark plug

1. Disconnect the spark plug lead. Then, clean the area around the spark plug to avoid getting debris in the combustion chamber when you remove the plug.

2. Remove the spark plug using a spark plug socket.

3. Clean light deposits from the plug with a wire brush and spray-on plug cleaner. Then, use a sturdy knife if necessary to scrape off tough deposits. NOTE: Never clean a spark plug with a shot blaster or abrasives.

4. Inspect the spark plug for very stubborn deposits, or for cracked porcelain or electrodes that have been burned away. If any of these condi-

tions exist, replace the spark plug.

5. Use a spark plug gauge to measure the gap between the two electrodes (one straight, one curved) at the tip of your spark plug **(photo A)**. Many small engines require a .030" gap. Check the specifications for your model with your power equipment dealer. If necessary, use a spark plug gauge to adjust the gap by gently bending the curved electrode. When the gap is correct, the gauge will drag slightly as you pull it through the gap.

6. Reinstall the plug, taking care not to overtighten. Then, attach the spark plug lead.

Checking ignition with a spark tester

A spark tester offers an inexpensive, easy way to diagnose ignition problems (see "Checking for Spark Miss"). If you find a problem, remove and inspect the spark plug. Replace the spark plug if you find evidence of wear or burning at the spark plug tip. Spark plugs are inexpensive and a new one may solve the problem.

1. Connect the spark plug lead to the long terminal of your tester and ground the tester to the engine with the tester's alligator clip **(photo B)**.

2. Use the rewind or electric starter to crank the engine, and look for a spark in the tester's window.

3. If you see a spark jump the gap in the tester, the ignition is functioning. The absence of a visible spark indicates a problem in the ignition system.

Checking for spark miss

A spark plug that is fouled or improperly gapped may not allow sparks to jump the gap between electrodes consistently. The spark plug will fire erratically or may occasionally fail to spark. Test for this problem—known as spark "miss"—if your engine stumbles, with a noticeable decrease in engine sound. Spark miss can also cause the engine to emit black smoke or a popping sound, as unburned fuel exits with the exhaust and ignites inside the muffler.

1. With the spark plug screwed into the cylinder head, attach the spark plug lead to the long terminal of the spark tester. Attach the tester's alligator clip to the spark plug **(photo C)**.

2. Start the engine and watch the tester's spark gap. You'll recognize spark miss by the uneven timing of the sparks in the tester.

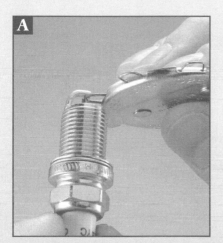

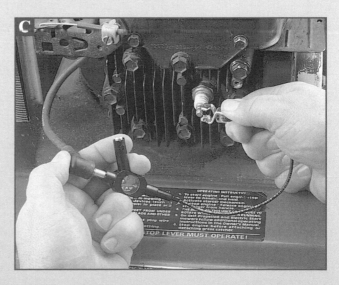

place when you bought the place, you will probably be tempted to stick with it rather than investing in a whole new system; however, dock design and hardware have improved in recent years. It might be worth your while to consider investing in a new dock system that is easier to put in and out.

Cleanup

A basic part of Opening Weekend is cleanup. If you cleaned while shutting down last season, this shouldn't be too hard. No matter how carefully you cleaned when closing down, you'll want to wash the windows and vacuum the place thoroughly.

Opening cleanup doesn't need much explanation. You clean windows and vacuum floors in vacation homes the same way you do in primary homes.

For washing windows, nothing beats the way the pros do it, with a squeegee. Buy a high quality squeegee, not a cheap one. Pour three tablespoons of ammonia in a bucket of warm (not hot) water. Pick a time to wash the windows when the sun won't be beating in on them. Wash the window with a sponge that has a white scrubbing surface (the green and pink are too abrasive). Wipe a dry strip on the top of the window, then pull your squeegee down smoothly. Use plenty of clean rags to dry the squeegee blade between strokes.

Sometimes it makes good sense to invest in a few products that will help you at cleanup time, such as vacuum hose extensions for reaching hard-to-get-to spots or maybe a quality stepladder with a big shelf on it to hold a bucket of suds. There is a huge differ-

ence in safety between working with a marginal, tipsy wood stepladder and a metal and nylon stepladder that is broad and stable.

A typical problem for owners of vacation properties is that they run out of some key product in the middle of the opening cleanup. Vacuum cleaner bags are a particular nuisance because backwoods general stores cannot be expected to stock bags for every type of vacuum cleaner on the market. In view of how cheap bags are and how hard they can be to find, it makes sense to buy so many you won't ever run out. I have a lifetime supply at my cabin.

Mouse cleanup

If your place has suffered an infestation of mice, the opening cleanup has to be fussier. Mice often carry a pulmonary disease called Hantavirus that can be fatal to humans. Hantavirus can be spread by contact with mouse poop or urine. Unfortunately, one of the most likely ways to contract the disease is by inhaling dust after cleaning mouse droppings, although handling dead mice is dangerous, too. That means if you just sail into a dirty room with a broom or vacuum cleaner, you are likely to stir up infected dust, and that can make you sick.

Handle mouse debris very carefully. Before you start cleaning, fill the cabin with fresh air by opening windows and doors. According to authorities, you shouldn't even occupy the house until it has aired for an hour.

When the air has been refreshed, clean up any mouse debris. Wear rubber or latex gloves and a respirator mask. Mix a solution of one cup of bleach to a gallon of water, or use a household disinfectant that is guaranteed to kill viruses. Do not vacuum or sweep mouse poop. Fill a spray bottle with your bleach solution and spray areas where you see droppings. Wipe down counter tops, cabinets and drawers with the disinfectant solution. Mop floors and baseboard areas with the bleach solution. Launder any upholstery or clothing items that mice have contacted. Carefully dispose of dead mice by handling them with gloves, dropping them into a resalable plastic bag. Place the bag containing the mouse into a second bag and seal it. Shower after conducting the cleanup.

RE-SUPPLY

After you have worked out a plan for your opening cleanup, make a list of the supplies you need. Take that list home and keep it in a safe place, such as in a computer file, in a card file or on a bulletin board. Modify it when you learn new and better ways of doing the cleanup. That list will make sure you will be prepared when you come up for future Opening Weekends.

You probably left the cabin pretty bare when you closed it down last fall. As you begin laying plans for a brand-new season of fun, it is time to restore your supplies of all the basic things you'll need. This, too, is easier if you make a list of the things you should check and possibly re-supply on Opening Weekend.

Some examples:

• Fill your gas cans with a fresh supply of gasoline. Keep the pure gasoline and gas/oil mix cans separate and clearly labeled.

• Fill any water jugs.

• Check propane tanks to see how full they are. If you are in doubt, ask for a service call to be sure you have a good supply. The best system involves two tanks with a valve that automatically flips when a tank goes dry. If you keep track of which tank you have been using, the flipped valve will be an obvious sign it is time to refill the empty tank. It is smart to keep a notebook in the cabin to keep track of when you get a fresh fill of propane. You don't want to start a vacation stay at the cabin and find that you are totally out of propane on a Sunday, with no immediate prospect of getting a refill.

• If you have lanterns that burn white gas, kerosene or lamp oil, be sure you have a good supply. If your cabin dinners feature a lot of romantic candlelight, use Opening Weekend to replenish your supply.

• Check your first-aid kit to make sure the essential supplies are all there. Check the cabinet for bug spray, bug lotion and sunscreen.

• If you use charcoal briquettes in your grill, check your supply. Briquettes can absorb humidity in muggy climates, so you might want to pitch out last year's briquettes and lay in a supply of fresh ones. Be sure you have starter fluid and wooden matches or a butane grill lighter with a long snout.

• Do you need to start up any seasonal subscriptions or services? Some families don't maintain telephone service in the off-season. Some families have the *New York Times* delivered on summer weekends. Now's the time to make arrangements.

You can build this firewood shed by following the directions on page 130.

FIREWOOD

Opening Weekend is a good time to order or cut next winter's supply of firewood. Wet, "green" firewood doesn't burn well and is hazardous because it can coat your chimney with layers of creosote that can lead to deadly chimney fires. Wood that is cut and split and appropriately stacked in spring will usually be in perfect shape to burn in fall and winter.

When you take stock of your supplies, don't forget that you'll want dry firewood in just a few months. If you cut, split and dry your own wood, now is the time to do it. If you buy firewood from local loggers, you might not need to worry about this in spring, for local loggers often sell their wood already aged and ready to use (but of course, you pay extra for that).

Firewood won't dry properly unless you handle it properly. The finer you split the wood, the more open surface you'll have for the green wood to shed moisture. If you store wood directly on the ground, the bottom layer often will stay wet and might even rot rather than drying. There is an art to stacking firewood in ways that are neat and which allow air to circulate. A stick of firewood exudes moisture in all directions, but mostly through the cut ends. Stack your wood so the ends can breath, then cover the top of the stack to protect the wood against rain but don't bundle up the whole stack in nylon or you'll slow the drying process needlessly. You can buy covers specifically built to fit a stack of firewood.

Woodsheds are usually built to keep firewood off the ground. If you stack your wood in the open, an inexpensive product will help you form neat stacks and promote drying. Some hardware stores and mail-order catalogs offer stacking frames that you attach to 2 x 4 timbers to make a simple framework to support a stack of firewood. Because some of the 2 x 4 frame pieces will be in contact with the ground, buy pressure-treated lumber for this use. Fireplace stores and mail-order catalogs also sell metal racks that will store your firewood neatly, keeping it off the ground.

Don't place firewood right next to your vacation home. Firewood stacks sometimes harbor critters—nasty bug critters or troublesome mammalian critters. A stack of wood in contact with the house invites those critters to come inside.

Many vacation homes have a woodshed or stacks of firewood stored about 30 feet away. Then the owners have a wood box or some sort of rack indoors to store enough wood to provide heat for a day. This arrangement makes it less likely that you'll have to dash out in a blizzard or heavy downpour to get wood, since you have just enough stored inside.

KITCHEN RE-SUPPLY

At the end of the season it isn't smart to leave food in the cabinets. Critters can get at rice, flour, crackers and cereals. Products with oil in them can emulsify in cold weather. Bottled goods freeze and explode. Canned goods can swell and take on spooky shapes. Salt can go hard in the shaker, forming a solid cake that will not come out no matter how hard you pound or flail the shaker. Curry and other spices can lose their zip after aging a few months, and any spice older than a year should be replaced.

Keep your inventory of food light and take most of it home at season's end. Opening Weekend is a good time to start anew. The cook can draw up a grand list of staples. That

ROMANTIC WEEKEND

A friend invited a new girlfriend to his cabin for a romantic north-woods getaway. He failed to consider the fact that the cabin had been sitting empty for months.

When the girlfriend walked in, she was hit by the stench of rotting mice. The cabin owner later determined that seven mice had died while the cabin had been unused. And of course, the windows were all shut tight, so the smell had nowhere to go.

Worse, an eighth mouse was in the act of dying as the girlfriend walked in. This mouse staggered around in circles on the kitchen rug, dying with the drama usually associated with Italian opera.

The romantic weekend did not go as planned.

first shopping trip of the season is great fun, for you are laying in the foundation for delicious meals prepared and enjoyed in your favorite spot on earth.

You can conduct this shopping trip at home and transport the groceries and other supplies on Opening Weekend. Most of us live close to larger population centers, where we enjoy lower prices and a better selection than we can find in stores close to our vacation homes. As a later chapter will explain, however, there is much to be said for purchasing as much of your shopping list as possible in the local community.

Once again, it is smart to make lists and keep them, modifying them over the years as experience teaches you what you really need and what just seems it might be nice to have. I keep lists on my computer because that is such a convenient way to store them and they can always be edited. Other systems work just as well. What doesn't work is having no system at all.

WHAT-TO-BRING

☐ **Cleaning supplies**
☐ Plastic trash bags
☐ Broom
☐ Mop
☐ Bucket
☐ Vacuum cleaner
☐ Dish soap
☐ Laundry soap
☐ Cleaning solutions
☐ _____
☐ _____
☐ _____

☐ **Kitchen supplies**
☐ Pots, pans
☐ Dishes
☐ Knives, spoons, forks
☐ Baking sheet
☐ Cups & glasses
☐ Serving platters
☐ Serving pitchers
☐ Paper plates, cups
☐ Thermos
☐ Picnic basket
☐ Cooler
☐ _____
☐ _____
☐ _____
☐ _____

☐ **Clothware**
☐ Dishcloths & towels
☐ Sheets
☐ Pillows
☐ Pillowcases
☐ Curtains
☐ Blankets
☐ Tablecloths
☐ _____
☐ _____
☐ _____

☐ **Food**
☐ Breakfast cereal
☐ Coffee, tea
☐ Milk, juice
☐ Bread, buns
☐ Canned goods
☐ Main dishes
☐ Sugar, salt, pepper
☐ Mustard, ketchup
☐ Drinking water
☐ Adult beverages
☐ _____
☐ _____
☐ _____

☐ **Recreational supplies**
☐ Books & magazines
☐ Hobby supplies
☐ Playing cards
☐ Board games
☐ Puzzle books
☐ Videos, DVDs, CDs
☐ Batteries
☐ _____
☐ _____
☐ _____

☐ **Toiletries**
☐ Toilet paper
☐ Prescription medicines
☐ Over-the-counter meds
☐ Pain medications
☐ Bath soap
☐ Shampoo
☐ Toothpaste, toothbrushes
☐ First-aid kit
☐ Insect repellant
☐ Sunscreen
☐ _____
☐ _____
☐ _____

☐ **Clothing**
☐ Socks, underwear
☐ Shorts, trousers
☐ Shirts, blouses
☐ Sweaters
☐ Jackets, coats
☐ Hats, gloves
☐ Rain gear
☐ Umbrella
☐ Swimsuits
☐ Shoes, sandals
☐ _____
☐ _____

☐ **Outdoor supplies**
☐ Charcoal & lighter
☐ Grill & accessories
☐ Fire extinguisher
☐ Lawn furniture
☐ Lawn games
☐ Boating items
☐ Lawn care tools
☐ Mower
☐ Pruning shears
☐ Rake
☐ Shovel
☐ Garden trowel

☐ **Basic tool kit**
☐ Hammer
☐ Pliers
☐ Screwdrivers
☐ Caulk gun
☐ Putty knife
☐ Drill & bits
☐ _____
☐ _____
☐ _____
☐ _____
☐ _____

AFTER-YOU-ARRIVE

☐ **Outside inspection**
- ☐ Are there any fallen tree branches?
- ☐ Is there brush to be cleared?
- ☐ Any invasive plants?
- ☐ Any broken windows?
- ☐ Storm damage to roof? Outbuildings?
- ☐ Check foundation for cracks

☐ **System startups**
- ☐ Turn on the circuit breakers
- ☐ Check to see if appliances run
- ☐ Plug in lamps, appliances
- ☐ Restore water supply
- ☐ Run water for 20 min. to clear pipes
- ☐ Open gas valves, if they are closed; inspect fittings for leaks
- ☐ Test furnace
- ☐ Change furnace filter, if necessary
- ☐ Inspect, service well pump, if needed
- ☐ Light or turn on water heater
- ☐ Check plumbing for leaks
- ☐ Check toilet, faucets for operation
- ☐ Check phones for operation
- ☐ Clean out fireplace or wood stove
- ☐ Open chimney dampers
- ☐ Check smoke detectors for operation

☐ **Interior inspection**
- ☐ Look for mice or insect infestation
- ☐ Uncover furniture, check upholstery
- ☐ Check ceiling for water damage
- ☐ Check window screens for holes
- ☐ Prioritize cleaning needs

☐ **Settling in**
- ☐ Delegate and complete cleaning tasks
- ☐ Stock food and kitchen supplies
- ☐ Store clothing and recreational gear
- ☐ Prepare hot tub or pool, if present
- ☐ Retrieve mail
- ☐ Let neighbors know you've arrived
- ☐ Check levels in LP or oil tanks; order replenishment if needed
- ☐ Check supply of lantern oil; resupply if needed
- ☐ Start up newspaper, magazine subscriptions, if necessary

☐ **Outdoor chores**
- ☐ Stow lawn and garden equipment
- ☐ Change oil, filters on lawnmower, chainsaw and other power equipment
- ☐ Test all power equipment
- ☐ Check gas supply
- ☐ Check firewood supply; restock as needed
- ☐ Inspect trash areas for animal activity; secure trash containers
- ☐ Install the dock, if applicable
- ☐ Launch and secure boat

- ☐ _____
- ☐ _____
- ☐ _____
- ☐ _____
- ☐ _____
- ☐ _____
- ☐ _____
- ☐ _____

CHAPTER 5
CRITTERS

T HE LIVES OF CONTEMPORARY AMERICANS
HAVE CHANGED OVER THE DECADES UNTIL
RELATIVELY FEW OF US HAVE MUCH CONTACT
WITH ANIMALS.

At one time most people worked on farms, rode horses and hunted.
Many people were sophisticated about animal behavior in the way
some are now sophisticated about shaving minutes off their daily commute by taking alternative routes. As a society, modern Americans
have a poor grasp of how animals operate. Some folks don't even have
enough contact with dogs or cats to be able to relate to them comfortably.

People from urban areas who purchase vacation property are often
unprepared for dealing with the wild animals they encounter there.
They typically buy their homes with hopes of observing wildlife, but
they are unprepared for the various ways critters can bedevil owners of
vacation property. They learn.

Increasingly, people tend to have one of three attitudes toward the animals they find on their land. One common attitude is "live and let live." People with this perspective feel friendly toward all animals. Finding ants in the kitchen, they wonder if there is any way to get rid of them without resorting to poison. When they see a raccoon in the shed, they are delighted and want to grab a camera. They love "nature," so when they spot animals on their land they are amused.

Another group of folks arrive with a deep, irrational fear of animals. The sight of a skunk throws them into panic. If a bear wanders past the cabin windows, they fear for their lives and phone the local game warden, asking that the intruder be shot. These folks reflexively think of any animal as a threat or a problem.

Watching wildlife can be one of the joys of owning a vacation home. Providing the right habitat—flowering plants to draw butterflies, for example—is a key to success.

Increasingly, new owners of recreational land arrive with romantic ideas about wildlife. They have had no contact with wildlife except as images on the television screen, where wildlife films present animals—even large predators—sympathetically. These people now have highly sentimentalized views about animals, seeing all wild creatures as something like friends or pets, and they are eager to show their good will toward animals.

There are risks involved with all three attitudes.

It isn't reasonable to fear all critters and try to exterminate them from your land. The raccoons and juncos and squirrels haven't moved several hundred miles to invade your lawn; you moved into their home territory. Your uninvited presence in wild areas might be a direct threat to the wildlife that has lived there for centuries.

You should strive to be a good neighbor, doing as little damage to the natural world as you can. A judicious amount of humility and tolerance are appropriate for anyone who buys vacation property. There is nothing immoral about buying recreational property, but each time another cabin, house or condo complex is erected in a formerly wild area, that area loses some of its wildness and the animals living nearby lose a little more living room. Strive to make your presence as benign as possible for the wildlife that has traditionally lived on your vacation property. Leave a small footprint on the local ecology.

Sadly, the most dangerous attitude toward wild critters is the sentimental, friendly one. Wild animals are wild. They aren't pets, and they haven't been put on earth to be your friends. Appreciating wildlife is a natural and attractive quality, but you should show your affection appropriately. That mostly means you shouldn't meddle in their lives, even if you mean the meddling to be positive for the animals involved.

There is nothing wrong with feeding birds if you do it properly, but feeding other forms of wildlife usually results in unnatural concentrations of those animals and can lead to trouble. Above all, it is criminally stupid to feed dangerous predators such as bears or wolves, encouraging them to make themselves visible for you. Any large predator that is fed is apt to lose its fear of humans. That animal is then doomed. Sooner or later, it will do something that will cause some human to kill it. The animal is not to blame for behaving naturally in an unnatural situation. The death of that formerly wild animal is strictly the fault of the uninformed (if well-intentioned) person who fed that animal.

The "live and let live" attitude toward wildlife is appropriately respectful and basically sensible. The problem is that wild critters naturally find human buildings attractive, and that can lead to big trouble. People often are dismayed to discover that they are obliged to wage a sort of war with animals to keep them out in the wild where they belong, not in the house or its associated outbuildings. "Live and let live" is a great goal so long as the critters stay on their side of the door and do no damage to your property. You should expect animals to do everything they can to share the lovely living space you have

created in their habitat, for houses are attractive sheltered environments and are usually full of food. Critters that destroy your property or invade your space require you to act.

City folks are often surprised to find that the laws regarding animal pests are loose in lightly settled areas. Some nuisance animals such as squirrels or raccoons are protected species whose taking is regulated by state law. As a practical matter, however, conservation officers in most areas expect homeowners to shoot nuisance animals—even protected species. There is even a name for this policy: "shoot, shovel and shut up."

The unwritten law in most vacation property areas is that landowners are expected to deal with nuisance animals quietly on their own without bothering authorities. There are not enough conservation officers on earth to chase down every raccoon and young bat that tries to set up housekeeping in an isolated vacation home. If you are dealing with a protected species that is damaging your property,

Mice can cause more damage than almost any other animal pest. They are also very hard to control.

RODENT RAGE

Mice begin coming indoors just about the same time most folks are closing up the vacation home for the season. More than one family has returned the following spring to find shredded paper littering the cupboards and closets, rodent droppings everywhere, and families of mice nesting within the cushions of furniture. Mice are incredibly resilient, and seem to find a way inside no matter what you do.

You can minimize mouse infestation by plugging every small hole and crack you can find, especially those in foundations and near the bottom of door frames.

Cracks need not be this big to allow mice to enter. This one is a veritable freeway for the rodent rushhour that occurs as weather cools in the autumn.

If you can't complete masonry patchwork immediately, stuff holes and cracks with fiberglass insulation or steel wool. It may not seem like much of a barrier, but rodents won't bite into these substances.

you should make a phone call before taking any action, but don't be shocked if the local conservation officer advises you to break the law as discretely as possible.

An exception would be a large animal, such as a bear. If you have bear problems, call a conservation officer. Shooting a bear on your land, even if you think you are operating in self defense, could bring you expensive legal problems. Moreover, shooting a bear can be risky. There are almost always better ways of dealing with troublesome bears, anyway.

MICE

If you have a mouse-proof place, count your blessings. Mice are amazingly adept at finding tiny cracks in foundations and walls. To a mouse, a vacation home must seem like heaven. It is warm and free of owls and weasels. It has unlimited food and nest-making materials. When autumn temperatures begin to dip, mice naturally try to find a way to get inside where they can be cozy and safe.

And when they want in, mice almost always can find a way. Most houses have several potential entry points, many of them located in spots only a mouse would know about. You aren't two inches high, and you don't routinely run around by the foundation, so you don't see the things that mice see. Buildings, especially cabins and cottages, are not solid, tight entities; they usually have a great many openings in the walls and floors, openings that let pipes or vents or electrical connections pass through. If one of those openings is just slightly larger than it needs to be, mice will use it as a doorway. If the framing has shifted on the foundation, there could be tiny cracks somewhere that mice will find. When age, weather or critters have created holes or cracks, they can become regular mouse highways.

The mouse most likely to plague cabin owners is the white-footed mouse, also called the deer mouse. There are several other types of field mice and voles, and all of them will try to live inside your vacation home if they possibly can. Other rodents (such as squirrels and chipmunks) will also try to get in your cabin. But mice, because they are so small and so doggone fertile, are the greatest nuisance.

Mice have been designed to slip through the tiniest opening. They can push their tapered heads through openings as small as a quarter of an inch—which is the diameter of a pencil. Mice are also terrific leapers—they jump up as high as twelve inches. From a running start, a mouse can leap gaps between objects three feet apart.

Once they get inside your vacation home, mice enthusiastically set about making more mice. Females give birth to four litters or more a year, each litter having three to five baby mice. Two mice turn into eight. Eight turn into thirty-six. Thirty-six turns into a smelly, dangerous mess. Each mouse is a poop factory, leaving 9,000 droppings in a month.

Additionally, mice will trash your home by shredding clothing, upholstery or paper in order to make their beds. Because mice foul their own beds, they often move on and make new ones. By nibbling the insulation

coating on wiring, mice can disable cars, riding mowers and snowmobiles.

You cannot tolerate mice. They will degrade your house and your possessions. They also threaten your health because they carry a class of disease known as Hantaviruses. You must do everything possible to keep mice out. Once they get in, you have no choice but to deal with them ruthlessly.

Mouse exclusion begins with a thorough inspection, particularly the foundation or where the foundation and the walls meet. Get down at mouse level to look for any tiny openings, including any little gap around wires, vents or pipes. Fill the openings with steel wool or expanding foam insulation from an aerosol can.

Do not attract mice by storing wood next to the house. Have all woodpiles 100 feet away, and minimize trash and brush near or under the house. You want the environment immediately around your cottage to be sterile and open, the sort of place tiny rodents avoid because they can be picked off easily there by predators.

Inside, keep all food in mouse-proof containers. Keep dog food in metal containers, like a metal garbage container with a lid that seals tightly. When you serve your dog, don't leave uneaten food on the floor but pour it back in that safe container. If you feed birds, store the seed in a metal container and police the area under your feeder so it doesn't accumulate a pile of seed that would attract mice. Keep your garbage in sealed containers, whether you have the garbage inside or outside. If you store food in cabinets, make sure the doors close tightly and firmly. In general, try to minimize the amount of food left around. At a year-round home you can stock all sorts of staples to use when the occasion arises. At a vacation property, that is risky unless you store the food in ways sure to defeat mice.

Once mice get in and begin multiplying, you have to go to war. Set traps in places where you find evidence of mouse activity. The classic mousetrap bait is peanut butter, but bacon grease is great. Some trappers like to feed the mice with traps that aren't set for a few days. Then when the mice have gotten bold, they arm all the traps. Place traps in dark areas and especially along walls, for mice tend to move right along walls. Mice like to have one side of their bodies in contact with a solid surface. Place your traps $\frac{1}{8}$ inch from walls, about six to eight feet apart, with the triggers placed toward the wall.

Experiment with different trap types and different baits. It is smart to use more than one trap type. Some large traps (sometimes called bait stations) will capture several mice at once. I find the idea creepy, but the sticky traps are reputed to be effective. If you have access to the Internet, enter "mouse control" in a search engine. You'll find many pages of products and suggestions.

Ultimately, nothing has worked as well as poison. I came to use poison reluctantly, but I once found my cabin overrun with mice that avoided my traps. I was so desperate, and the mice were so bold that one night I shot a bunch of them with a pellet pistol. I

finally solved that problem by putting down poison. I no longer hesitate to use poison. Do what you have to do, but do it in a way that protects children and pets.

SQUIRRELS

Squirrels, for all practical purposes, are jumbo mice. That actually makes them easier to deal with since they are easier to exclude, although a squirrel can make a mighty big mess if it nests indoors.

Keep squirrels out by blocking any potential holes. Because they are climbers, you'll have to worry about high holes, like any opening under the eaves or behind the fascia board. Squirrels generally need an opening the size of a golf ball to get in. You often know you have squirrels when you find stockpiles of nuts or other food items. They also shred upholstery or fabrics to make nests. Their nests are usually large and conspicuous.

If you find squirrels in residence in your house or one of your outbuildings, throw open the windows and doors and make the place as bright as possible. The squirrels are almost sure to leave during the daylight hours. When you're sure the squirrel is gone, close up the hole. The classic aid for closing holes in outbuildings is hardware cloth. Staple it firmly in place, overlapping the hole by a large margin. Squirrels will chew wood to enlarge an opening, and they can be persistent once they've learned how nice life is inside your cabin.

BATS

Thinking about bats has changed radically in recent years. People used to fear them hysterically. Many a poor bat has been whacked to death with a tennis racket for no good reason. Bats have a bad reputation because they sometimes carry rabies. In point of fact, rabies is rare among bats. And then there are all those old wives' tales about bats flying into women's hair and getting tangled there. Some people just find bats spooky.

But new thinking is changing attitudes. Many people now actually encourage bats to live nearby. And no wonder: Bats live exclusively on a diet of insects. A single brown bat can ingest over a hundred mosquitoes an hour. After you have swatted enough mosquitoes, you might join the large group of people who see bats as valuable allies in the never-ending war against bugs. Several mail-order catalogs and web sites now sell bat houses. Prices run from about $30 to $90, which is one indication of how determined some people are to attract bats to their vacation properties.

If you want to attract bats, do some research. The Internet is a great resource for information about the design and mounting of bat houses. Some designs are better than others, and there is quite a bit to know about where to locate a house to maximize the chances it will actually attract bats. Of course, anyone trying to sell you something is a biased source of information. For untainted advice, check your extension division or look up the Internet pages maintained by the Organization for Bat Conservation.

As desirable as bats are around your property, you don't want bats in your home. They

Apply silicone caulk around dryer and fan vents and any other fittings mounted on the outside of your house.

Use sprayable foam insulation to seal the air gaps around spigots and other exterior entry points.

Close up the gap between the house sill and the siding by stuffing it with caulking backer rope.

Bats are good when they're outside eating insects, not so great if they invade your home. To prevent their invasion make sure all vent openings have wire mesh or screening over them.

will squeak and rustle and annoy you with their droppings. It is generally juvenile bats that break into houses. They don't know better, and once they've experienced the panic of encountering you in the house they probably won't return if you let them out.

Inspect your house in the fall, for all bats should have left your home by then. Look for entry points. Holes will often be surrounded by a smeary ring of debris. Bats often come in right at the joint of roofs and walls, behind the fascia, or through broken attic vents or any other cracks. Sometimes bats come down the chimney. Mice enter cabins through low cracks; bats come inside through high cracks. Bats can squeeze through a crack the diameter of a ballpoint pen.

When you identify the way bats have been

getting in your cabin, encourage them to leave and then close the opening. Use nylon net, steel wool, hardware cloth or boards to seal the opening.

If a bat does get inside, there is no reason for panic and certainly no reason to kill it. Open windows and doors to encourage it to leave. It helps to close off all rooms except the one where the bat is. Turn down the lights so the room isn't so dark the bat wants to hide from the light. Open the windows and sit there calmly watching until the bat leaves. It isn't as likely to fly if you are moving around.

If you have to trap a bat, place a coffee can or large bowl over the bat. Slide a piece of cardboard under the container. Liberate it outside without touching it with your bare hands. If the bat appears sick, do not release it. If a bat manages to bite or scratch someone, trap it and kill it so authorities can check it for rabies.

If bats have been nesting in your home, open doors and windows and dump naphthalene balls (mothballs) in their nesting area. You might make them feel unwelcome by shining a bright light in their nesting area. They'll usually leave on their own, after which you can seal any holes. Keep a good cap on your chimney.

SKUNKS

Skunks are gentle creatures that actually do a lot of good by eating insects and small rodents that might otherwise be trying to break into your cabin. They can carry rabies and distemper, which is mostly a threat to unvaccinated pets. Obviously, all pets have to be vaccinated against rabies, whether or not they ever travel to wild areas. But because a threatened skunk can defend itself in such a smelly way, few people want to coexist with skunks.

Avoid attracting skunks to your land. You already know you should never store dog food outside or leave your garbage in a way that attracts critters. Keep the area around the house clean and open. If you have outbuildings, place hardware cloth around the base of the structure to prevent skunks from taking up residence there.

If you need to get rid of a skunk that is living on your land, buy one of those live traps. A can of meaty cat food makes excellent bait. Place the trap near the den entrance or the place you most often see the skunk coming and going. When you get a skunk, approach the trap calmly and place a heavy cloth covering over the trap. You can now usually transport the skunk to a distant location. Believe it or not, if you release a skunk closer than ten miles away, it might find its way back. As slow as they are, skunks are stubborn, and they'll keep strolling until they get back home unless you move them at least ten miles away.

If you feel you absolutely must kill the skunk, drop the trap and the skunk into water to drown it. But try to be tolerant. Skunks are slow, mellow and generally unthreatening. You just don't want them living on your land.

HERE, KITTY, KITTY!

Skunks have amiable dispositions, possibly because Mother Nature gave them such excellent protection that they have had no need to be aggressive. Some people even buy de-scented skunks as pets. That's usually a mistake, for skunks have not been altered by many generations of special breeding to have personalities most people can live with. They are stubborn and inclined to get in trouble. But the wild ones are generally placid, not looking for trouble.

A family I know once went camping at a state campground where skunks had learned they could find food at night by rooting around the campground in the dark. The family—a father, mother and two sons—was sleeping in a large wall tent.

The mother was awakened by the sound of her younger son's voice.

"Nice kitty," he said, over and over. "You are such a nice kitty."

It didn't seem likely to her that a cat would be wandering a state campground deep in a pine forest. When she found a flashlight, she confirmed her worst fear. The "kitty" was a skunk. Her son was holding it to his chest, stroking it.

She was able to gently separate her son from the wild "kitty" and ease it out the tent door. The experience, however, rattled her and convinced the family to switch to camping in a travel trailer.

RACCOONS

Raccoons are smart and persistent burglars. Like bears, they are omnivores, meaning they'll eat almost anything or everything. Like skunks, they are mostly nocturnal. In general, raccoons are a junior version of a black bear. Coons can test the intelligence and patience of owners of recreational property. They do get rabies, although quite rarely. The scat of raccoons is particularly nasty and inclined to harbor parasites. They

Raccoons are incredibly ingenious when it comes to getting at food.

also carry distemper, which is a reminder of the need to keep your pets immunized.

The three main ways raccoons create trouble are by breaking into your cottage, by raiding the garbage and by filching produce food from gardens. If you mean to grow sweet corn in raccoon territory, you'll have to erect a tight fence to keep raccoons and deer out. You might even need to electrify the fence at night to keep the coons at bay. The best electric fence has hot wire strung at five and twelve inches. Your local DNR or extension division will have details.

There are many products that are supposed to frighten or drive raccoons away by being obnoxious. Unfortunately, these wily critters quickly learn to ignore the things humans put out to repel or frighten them. You don't want to get into a battle of wits with raccoons. It is rough on the human ego.

The best advice with respect to raccoons is to keep a tight rein and button down your garbage so coons never come to think of your place as a food station. Uncapped chimneys are a common entry point. A heavy wire mesh cap will stop raccoons, however. Never leave pet food out where it could attract raccoons. Store garbage inside or in tough, locking metal or nylon containers.

If raccoons take up residence in your house or outbuildings, you could try to deal with them yourself, but that's not always a winning strategy. You can sometimes drive raccoons away from their nests if you sprinkle mothballs around, turn on bright lights and leave a loud radio playing. Leave an exit for the coons. If they do leave, seal up any holes and clean up the mess.

But raccoons can be persistent. You might have to contact the local conservation officers to see what advice or help they can offer. Raccoons are a classic example of the sort of problem you want to avoid with prevention rather than solving by seeking a cure.

PORCUPINES

Porcupines are inherently funny and fun to watch. They used to enjoy a special sort of protection by wilderness travelers who valued porcupines as a food source of last resort in case they ever were trapped in the woods. But porkies do at least three things that give cabin owners headaches. They are attracted to the glue in plywood, and often eat large areas of fresh plywood. They dearly like the taste of salt, which is why they often chew the handles of axes and other tools. Worse, they girdle and kill trees.

The first time I encountered a porcupine on my land, I was delighted. Within days, I watched two porkies kill four large trees. With great reluctance, I brought a rifle on my next trip to the cabin. Earlier generations of porkies have defaced the plywood around my cabin.

To protect your home and outbuildings, erect a barrier of hardware cloth. Porkies are not great leapers, so the barrier only needs to be about 16 inches high. Keep brush and clutter away from the area right around the house or under it, if you have a crawl space. An open, sterile environment will discourage a great many critters—including mice, squirrels, chipmunks and porcupines—from spending a lot of time near the foundation.

If you have to trap a porkie, use one of those humane wire mesh traps. They are widely available at hardware stores in vacation country. Bait it with—believe it or not—strips of absorbent wood or a sponge soaked in salt water. When you get your porkie, take it for a long ride. You don't want to release it

Bears aren't just a wilderness phenomenon anymore. In many regions, bears routinely wander into the outskirts of major cities, so your chances of encountering one may be better than you think. The biggest threat from bears is not from physical attack, but damage they can do to your home trying to reach food.

ABBY'S BEARS

The bears that hit our cabin were known as "Abby's bears." Abby has a cabin about a mile from ours. Through a simple accident, these bears found food at her place. When they kept returning, Abby called for help. Authorities trapped the bears and relocated them, but the bears came back and raided Abby's cabin again. By the time they found my place, this gang had broken into Abby's place four times.

Abby's bears were a family of a mother and three cubs. This mother had the terrible luck of giving birth to three cubs in the winter of 1998, a winter that was followed by a summer of severe drought. Bears eat anything and everything, but just at summer's end they depend on fattening up on a feast of berries so they can survive the long winter of hibernation. The berry crop totally failed to appear in the summer of 1998. A mama bear desperate for food learned that cabins are full of food.

I took the phone call from my friend, Harold, who phoned to report that my cabin had been trashed by Abby's bears. A neighbor had sealed up the hole in the cabin door, but I was told to expect a nasty mess when I came up to clean up the cabin.

The mother bear had apparently held the screen door open with one arm while using the other to bash a hole in the front door. That door, a cheesy thing made of thin plywood and cardboard spacers, was so fragile I could have pushed my own fist right through it. That door offered no obstacle to the bears. I have no guess how long the four bears spent in the cabin.

When I got there days later to clean up the mess, so much trash covered the floor that when I walked around my shoes never touched the floor. I was walking on spilled food, broken lamps, smashed cabinets, empty food containers, ripped clothing and pieces of what had been beloved cabin objects. The bears went right to the refrigerator, tore it apart and munched on the fruit bin, both the plastic bin and its contents. They raided cabinets in order to mix together molasses, flour, soy sauce and rice. This mixture was now spread all over the debris on the floor. There were bear paw prints on the furniture. For reasons best known to bears, they had even chomped on my telephone, destroying it. To add insult to injury, one of the bears left a big gooey pile of poop by one of the windows.

The last person to use the cabin had left the cobs from a sweet corn dinner in the biffy, figuring that was a safe place. After all, who would open a locked outhouse door to see if there was food inside? But the bears smelled the cobs, and they knew how to deal with doors. Abby's bears tore apart the biffy's contents the same way they had rearranged the contents of my poor cabin.

In my first day of cleaning up, I filled sixteen trash bags with debris. At the end of three days of cleaning, I had things mostly in order. A local handyman mounted a metal door on the cabin and replaced the outhouse door. Many years after the bear attack, some things have still not been restored to the condition they were in before the bears had their party.

The saddest thing of all, actually, was the fate of the bears. Deciding that this gang was "incorrigible," the authorities trapped them again. They destroyed—shot—the mama bear and relocated the cubs. It isn't easy being a bear, even if you know everything there is to know about where to find food. I doubt the cubs survived much longer. But then, their fate was sealed the day their mother learned about all the food to be found behind Abby's cabin door.

within ten miles of your property. Like skunks, porcupines are slow walkers but stubborn about returning to lands they know.

BLACK BEARS

The bear that plagues cottage owners all across America these days is the black bear. Black bears are usually black with a small white chest patch but a few are brown. They are generally shy and reclusive. Black bears climb trees readily. Adult males weigh 200 to 500 pounds; females are significantly smaller and might not reach 200 pounds. Black bears are often described as "big, black eating machines." Black bears are quite a different animal from grizzlies, which are much larger and more aggressive. You've surely heard stories of bears attacking and killing people. With very few exceptions, those stories dealt with grizzlies, not black bears.

The status of black bears has changed in a major way in the past several decades. One result of that change is that black bears are both more numerous and more of a problem for vacation homeowners. Apart from pesky insects, the most difficult animals vacation property owners deal with are the smallest (mice) and largest (black bears).

Traditionally, people feared bears and often killed them on sight. Bears occupied the ambiguous and undesirable status of "varmints." Varmints are animals considered so lacking in value that they are legally unprotected and usually killed whenever the occasion permits. Many states have redefined black bears as big game animals that can only be taken during controlled seasons and

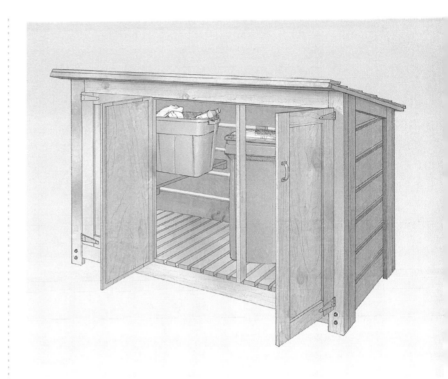

Keep garbage and recyclables sealed and hidden to thwart bears and other animals. To build this trash garage, see page 130.

in particular ways. At the same time, a great many people have learned that black bears rarely threaten humans.

Both changes have encouraged bear numbers to rise. Some observers thought classifying bears as big game animals might reduce bear numbers by over-harvesting them. Just the opposite has happened. It is difficult to hunt bears. Not enough bears are being harvested to maintain stable populations. For example, in the Northeast, bear complaints increased three hundred percent in one decade. Much the same thing is happening all across the nation.

Most bears are big sissies that fear us more than we fear them. A youngster with a pot and a spoon can usually send the biggest black bear fleeing in panic. Bears do kill a small number of humans each year, but the

BEAR ATTACKS

You needn't be afraid to move in bear country. Black bears are so timid that they almost always skedaddle when they encounter a human. Contrary to mythology, black bears are not even aggressive if you get between the mother bear and her cubs. It isn't smart practice, but black bears are rarely aggressive, even if the cubs seem threatened.

And yet bears do sometimes attack humans. It is rare, but it happens.

If you encounter a bear in a situation where the bear feels threatened and unable to escape, it might attack. Almost all attacks are bluffs. The bear will charge and make a lot of noise, but it is trying to scare you off, not hurt you. Stand your ground, and then calmly retreat while watching the bear.

In the extremely unlikely event of a real bear attack, don't play dead. Fight back. Fighting a grizzly only makes the griz meaner, but if you beat up on a black bear it will probably back off. Pepper spray will effectively deter black bears.

I once nearly stepped on a bear as I walked between my cabin and the nearby gazebo. The bear scuttled up a big balsam tree. Because I was in the gazebo, some ten feet from the tree, this poor bear was afraid to come down again. The bear couldn't decide what to do. It tried to spook me into leaving by making loud huffing sounds and chattering its teeth at me. Then, having threatened me, it would often bawl for help in a way that was both sad and funny.

I had trouble falling asleep for laughing that night at this bear that kept switching messages: "I'm gonna GET you!" And then, moments later, "MAMA! MAMA!" "I'm gonna GET you!" "MAMAAAAAAAAA!"

number is extremely low, particularly in view of how much contact bears and people have these days.

The real threat of bears is that they are learning to use houses as a source of food. Bears eat seed from bird feeders. If someone puts out corn to attract deer or squirrels, bears will often find it instead. Bears are learning to tear apart garbage cans to get at the food there. Bears attracted to food or garbage often discover that they can break into the house and find more food.

Bears eat almost everything imaginable. They have to. They're large animals and must eat a great deal. A mama bear with three or four cubs needs an astonishing amount of food to keep the whole gang going, and she is obliged to spend all of her waking hours foraging for food. Food can be abundant at various times of the year, but there are often critical moments when food becomes scarce. That's when the bear's keen nose is apt to attract it to human dwellings and human garbage containers.

You cannot get sloppy and let bears discover that your property is a great source of food. Any time bears find food in houses, their outbuildings or garbage containers, those bears lose their innocence and start haunting similar properties all the time. These bears don't live long. The lucky ones get trapped and relocated. Any bear that persists in foraging around humans is likely to be shot. The classic phrase in bear country is "a fed bear is a dead bear." It doesn't matter whether you feed a bear on purpose to enjoy watching it or by accident by storing food carelessly, the result is the same for the bear.

If you use your property sporadically, the best system is probably to keep smelly garbage indoors until you leave. Your house and garage should have bear-proof doors, preferably metal doors. Take all food scraps home with you to dispose of them where bears will never be an issue. If you store smelly garbage around your vacation property, bears will find it sooner or later, and then they'll use their enormous strength and intelligence to test the security of your containers. It is no longer appropriate to maintain compost piles in some rural areas because rotting vegetation attracts bears.

An Internet search will lead you to several sources of "bear-proof" or "bear-resistant" food and garbage containers. It takes a robust container to thwart a hungry bear. If you must store smelly garbage outside, keep it away from the house itself and enclose it in a bear-proof enclosure. That enclosure doesn't have to be pretty. An inexpensive cinderblock structure with a solid metal door will work. Additionally, many cottage owners like to sprinkle ammonia or camphor disks (sold in some drugstores) over garbage to reduce the allure of good smells. Do not burn food scraps. Burning garbage often intensifies the odors that attract bears. Although the thought is disgusting, one type of waste you shouldn't store casually outside is a soiled baby diaper. Bears are ravenous, the very opposite of picky eaters.

Keep your outdoor grill clean. Charcoal grills usually burn at high temperatures after the meat has been cooked, so they do a better job of incinerating grease and bits of food stuck to the grill than most gas grills. In that sense, charcoal grills are more suitable than gas grills if bears live near your property.

Bears have almost put an end to bird feeding in many areas, which is a sad loss. Bears, in spite of their vast bulk, mostly eat small food items, such as ants, berries, acorns, seeds, grubs and so forth. People who put out bird feeders are often astonished that such a bulky animal would be drawn to bird seed, but for a bear a full bird feeder is a big meal. If you leave full bird feeders around to attract birds, you'll sooner or later attract bears, and then you will have taught the bears that your property holds more of that wonderful food.

You still can feed the birds. Bears are mostly nocturnal. You can have bird feeders out at window level during the daylight hours if you monitor them and make sure no bears are using them as snack bars. Mount your feeders on thin ropes and pulleys. Lower the feeders during the day so they are low enough for you to fill and so you can enjoy watching the birds appreciate your food. Toward dark, run the feeders up high into the trees where bears can't get at them.

The best bear policy, in short, is an extreme form of sanitation that minimizes odors and prevents wandering bears from getting food in or near your property. If you slip up just once, you might teach a bear that your house is a source of food. That could

In many regions, deer are so plentiful that they are something of a nuisance. They can do incredible amounts of damage to gardens, landscapes and small trees, so be careful about courting their visits.

lead to agony for you or for some other homeowner, and it almost surely portends the eventual death of that bear.

DEER

The white-tailed deer is one of the most valued and enjoyed animal species in North America. Deer attract hunters who spend money in remote country. They provide food for local hunters. At all times of year, their graceful beauty is a joy to watch.

In many areas, however, people are beginning to wonder if they don't have too much of a good thing. State game agencies have lost the ability to control some regional white-tail populations. No matter how they

adjust the deer hunt regulations, hunters don't kill enough deer to keep the population in balance with the environment. This might be due to a trend toward milder winters, which in turn might represent one effect of global warming. That's speculative. Less controversial is the fact that fewer people are killing deer illegally—the formerly common practice of "poaching" that was common a few decades ago.

Deer numbers are reaching or breaking modern record levels in many areas. One consequence is that driving is becoming hazardous in many regions, particularly during the nighttime hours. Deer-auto collisions are common, expensive and sometimes tragic.

Owners of vacation property are sometimes tempted to feed deer. It isn't difficult. A crib filled with field corn will draw deer in. Natural resource departments advise against feeding deer. Feeding by humans can encourage local deer populations to rise steeply and get out of balance with the carrying capacity of the habitat. Wildlife experts also worry that artificial feeding like this concentrates deer and increases the probability that deer will pass diseases from one to another. Currently, several states are very concerned about CWD (chronic wasting disease), which is one strong reason for not creating conditions that concentrate deer.

Rural property owners often have to wage a running battle with deer to preserve trees. To keep a healthy number of trees growing, it is often necessary to plant young ones to replace those mature trees you are losing to storms. Deer often kill these young trees faster than you can plant them. The answer is to plant the tree and then completely surround it with protective wire mesh. You might need to increase the size of the wire barrier until the tree is big enough to survive without protection.

INSECT PESTS

There are a number of insect pests that take some of the fun out of owning recreational property. Everyone knows how annoying mosquitoes, black flies, ticks, deer flies and other insects can be. But some bugs represent a different kind of threat because they actually damage your property. Carpenter ants, termites, sawyer beetles and other wood-eating bugs are a threat to any building's integrity.

Getting rid of insects is tricky. My suggestion is that you take careful notes about what you are seeing the bugs do. If you spot sawdust, take notes about exactly where you find it. If at all possible, gather a specimen of the bug, either in adult or pupal form. Consult a specialist in nuisance insects. Your local DNR or extension division might be a resource. Talk to other people in the area to learn if this bug is something they've dealt with. Then decide if you can solve the problem yourself or if you need to call in professional help. Some insect problems can only be solved with chemicals that average folks aren't qualified to use.

In some areas with high numbers of cabins, professional exterminating services will take on insects and other critters that threaten vacation properties. Owners subscribe to the service, paying for an agent to periodically visit the properties to deal with problems that might be occurring there.

PEST CONTROL

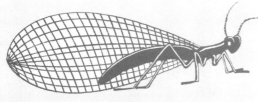

Lace Wing

Spider

Praying Mantis

Ladybug Beetle

While they are annoying and just plain creepy, not all pests pose any real risk to you or your home. In fact, some actually help: ladybugs and ladybird beetles eat the bugs that destroy your plants; lacewings eat a number of destructive bugs, including insect eggs; and spiders eat the bad bugs you don't want around (unfortunately, they eat the good ones, too). Other helpful insects include lightning bugs, dragonflies, and praying mantises.

However, there are a number of pests that can cause you potentially serious health problems and even compromise the structural integrity of your home. A fungus that grows on bat and bird droppings causes a respiratory disease called histoplasmosis; hantavirus is spread through mouse droppings; and cockroach feces are strongly linked to the rising asthma rates in children. And let's not forget about termites—these charming insects actually eat wood and can severely damage or weaken structural framing members.

The first step in combating pest infestation is to find the source of the problem. Examine the outside walls of your house—from the foundation up to the roof—and seal any cracks or holes that could allow insects or other pests inside. Pay particular attention to trails leading up to a crack or hole—more than likely, they are favorite and oft-used entrances for pests.

Gable vents are a common entry point for birds and bats. Place screening or 1/2-inch mesh hard-

ware cloth over these on either the inside or outside. Seal gaps between soffits and walls with trim molding, and trim any tree or shrub branches that touch or come close to the house or roofline. If you have a woodburning stove or fireplace, store wood away from the house. Woodpiles are havens for insects and other creatures.

It is best to leave any bird or bat droppings undisturbed. If you must clean the area, moisten the droppings first so they do not release dust. Do not use a shop vacuum to clean up droppings, as the filter will not catch the fungal particles and will thus spread them. If you choose to vacuum the area, use only a vacuum with a HEPA filter. Wear a respirator and disposable rubber gloves and wash all clothing in hot water immediately afterward.

Whenever you clean up mouse droppings or nesting materials, wear a respirator and disposable rubber gloves. Be careful not to touch your eyes, nose or mouth with the gloves. Dispose of the gloves after use.

It may not be possible to remove cockroach feces and shed cuticles because they tend to collect in hard-to-reach crevices. It's best to focus on eliminating the roach infestation. Because roaches do not like traveling in the open, an effective deterrent is to caulk or seal all potential travel paths. Use expanding foam to seal around all plumbing and utility line openings. Use clear or paintable caulk to seal around cabinets where they meet each other and the walls, and to seal baseboards where they meet at the floor and the wall. Eliminate the roaches by using bait stations or baiting gel. Don't use fogging devices, as these chemicals degrade interior air quality and are no more effective than bait stations. Prevent roach infestations by removing all food waste immediately and keeping surfaces clean. Follow these same techniques for handling ant infestations.

Dry, pest-free lumber will last for centuries, but wood attacked by rot or termites can be destroyed in short order. Framework at the foundation is the most vulnerable because it's so close to the ground. Act quickly if that lumber is damp or you suspect termites.

If you have reason to suspect termites, probe into the lumber with a penknife and flashlight. Termites destroy lumber by eating it from the inside out: Boards can be nearly hollow and still look fine on the surface.

Subterranean termites avoid light and open air. This common species tunnels up from the ground directly into the wood. They also can create

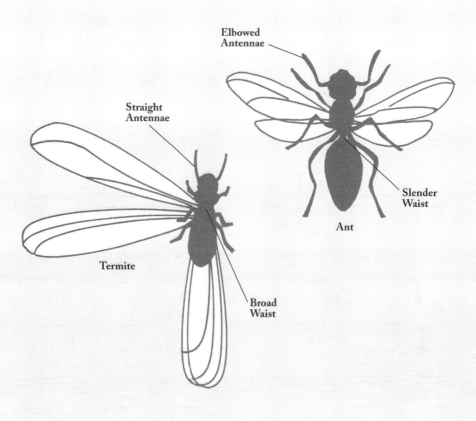

tunnels up foundation walls to reach wood framing.

Damp-wood termites live along the Pacific Coast. They damage only moisture-soaked wood.

Dry-wood termites, present in warm climates, bore directly into above-ground wood then cover their tracks by plugging their holes.

Carpenter ants are found in many of the same regions as termites, and the two are easily confused. Ants nest in wood but don't feed on it; so they do less damage than termites.

Call a reputable exterminator if you find insects. Most insecticides are very dangerous and difficult to apply. Rot can be just as damaging, but it's easier to guard against. Plug leaks, keep exterior caulk in good shape, and make sure the house is

adequately ventilated.

If you wind up with critters nesting in your home, immediately contact a pest-control specialist or your local animal control department. These individuals are trained to remove animals humanely and can provide information for preventing future pest problems.

CHAPTER 6

NETWORKING WITH THE LOCAL COMMUNITY

NEW PURCHASERS OF VACATION PROPERTY ARE OFTEN SLOW TO PERCEIVE THAT THEY HAVEN'T JUST BOUGHT A SECLUDED PLACE IN THE WOODS; THEY HAVE ALSO JOINED A COMMUNITY.

It is probably natural for people who have just bought a place to give little thought to the folks living in the area. The new owner will be totally absorbed with the property, dreaming of what fun the family can have there and what modifications they might want to make. When looking for vacation property, most people seek remoteness—a place where they can "get away from it all." They seek places where there aren't many people and where the natural world has not been heavily developed. Compared to a modern metro area, that vacation property often seems akin to wilderness.

Still, there are people around. The closest neighbors might not live right in sight, but they'll certainly think of you as a neighbor even if their place is half a mile down the mountain from yours. There are probably people living in the nearby community who have spent time on the land you bought. Many folks in the area probably remember the previous owner. Most local folks noticed when the bright signs went up listing the property for sale. When the signs came down, some local residents probably speculated about what you and your family would be like.

You are not anonymous to them in the same way they are anonymous to you at first. You will be identified provisionally as "the guy from Madison who bought the old Randolph place." You will later acquire a richer identity based on how you conduct yourself. Don't make the mistake of thinking you are anonymous or that your presence is unnoticed. To you, it might seem like "nobody" lives near your new property. But people in the area will be aware of you. They'll quietly track your comings and goings, and they will trade observations after you've gone home again.

The communities in lands blessed with recreational property tend to be tiny, with a tightly integrated social structure. It is often said that in a small town "everybody knows everybody else's business," and that's one of those clichés that can be literally true. People in small towns and lightly settled backcountry know each other with the intimacy and depth that only comes from spending many decades together. Indeed, quite often folks in tiny towns and rural areas remember the parents and grandparents of their neighbors. Their view of community is considerably richer and more personal than the view of most metropolitan dwellers.

While the people living near your place might seem unimportant to you when you first arrive, you need to understand that you are possibly someone of great interest to them. You have entered their community. Those folks will likely have strong feelings about their community, and they'll be watching you to see how well you will blend in.

FITTING IN

People who have owned vacation property for a while often discover to their surprise that one of the most enjoyable parts of the experience is getting to know the local citizens. Many find that they can't imagine how they would have gotten by without the generosity and wisdom of their local friends.

In spite of some possibly inaccurate connotations, let's use the word "locals" to refer to those folks who live full time in vacation property areas. They are the folks who manage the local motel. They are the proprietors of the gift shop. They are the people who cook at the café down the road from your place. You are one of those people who come and go. They might lump you in the general category of "summer people" if your vacation lies in lands not used much in winter. Unlike you, the locals live there all the time.

Locals are often uncomfortably aware of the fact that they live on the margins of American society. When they watch television, they rarely see characters or settings that remind them of their own lives. The evening news will rarely if ever show film of anything happening close to where they live. They typically have strong feelings of disconnectedness regarding international events, national politics and state government. When you talk to them, you get the feeling that they see themselves living almost in a different country from people in metro areas. Their focus is often intensely local.

Their reactions to living in a small, remote town might be complex. They might joke about what it is like to live in a town too small to support even one convenience store. Behind the joking, you may detect some fierce pride in their beautiful area. And if you scratch a little deeper, you might glimpse sensitivity about how inconsequential and anonymous their town is in the eyes of outsiders. The locals in vacation areas are frequently misunderstood, underestimated and ignored. On some days that will strike them as funny, and on others it will not.

It almost seems to be a basic economic law: if an area is beautiful and lightly developed, it will be difficult to make a living there. People who live in such areas rarely can support themselves with a single job. Working at two, three or four jobs is quite normal. One fellow in the little village near my cabin is a potter, a tax assessor, a carpenter and the proprietor of an antique store. When you buy milk and a newspaper in the morning, the sale might be rung up by the same young woman who serves your meal six hours later when you come into town for a restaurant meal. Most jobs pay poorly, so people scramble by putting together a variety of jobs.

Foster first-name relationships with local shop owners in the nearest community. They can be a valuable source of information and help.

If you own recreational land, you are almost surely much wealthier than the folks who live near your place. Many local residents in undeveloped country have no regrets about living in a beautiful area where wages are low. Some have consciously made that tradeoff. Others can be a little defensive, expecting outsiders to look down upon anyone who works so hard to make so little money. Perhaps you are too sensitive to be condescending toward people who struggle to make ends meet. Still, you should remember that some local people might assume that you feel superior to them.

Weather means something different to the locals in vacation country than to visitors. Regions where there is a great deal of vacation property live and die by the money that comes in when "the summer people" and tourists show up. In the little town near my cabin, things are so slow in the off-season that you might see a dog sleeping in the main street. When Memorial Day comes, the whole area comes to life as the summer people start showing up. Soon afterward, tourists begin filing through. Locals nervously monitor the weather. A summer of delightful weather keeps the cash registers singing, whereas a cold or rainy summer might put a few marginal shops right out of business.

What does all of this mean for the owner of recreational property? If you act superior or condescending, you make local people uncomfortable. On the other hand, if you treat them with the respect that all people deserve, they'll notice. Take an interest in their lives. Learn their names and use them. Ask questions about the history of the area.

Get to know neighbors, especially those that live in the area year-round. A neighbor who will keep an eye on your property while you're gone is a good friend to have.

If you approach local residents with sincere interest, you'll be richly rewarded.

You probably weren't thinking about joining a community when you bought that land. In fact, quite the opposite: you may have been thinking about getting away from people. But if you miss the chance to know the distinctive people living near you, you will be poorer for it.

PRECIOUS INFORMATION

You can benefit from the friendly assistance of local residents more than you would ever guess.

Local residents know the local weather. Many recreational property areas are located in country where weather can be extreme (deep snow close to Lake Superior, bitter cold in the mountains, hurricanes in seashore areas, etc.). Newcomers don't know what to expect of weather. More importantly, they don't know what practical measures to take to protect their property from extreme weather. The locals know.

In many regions rich with vacation land, the locals primarily heat their homes with wood. Wood stoves heat a great many recreational homes, too, although their owners rarely know what they are doing. The locals know which local woods burn best, who sells dry firewood at reasonable prices and who could scrub the creosote out of your chimney. Heating with wood seems romantic until you have tried it. People who have lived with wood heat have much to teach you.

DUMPMASTER JIM

The little town near my northern Wisconsin cabin used to have a landfill dump that was open twice a week. Presiding over the dump was the official dumpmaster, Jim. Jim was a semi-retired farmer who had served in France in World War II. He was a large man—some might say "fat"—and he wore pinstriped overalls and rubber boots.

When you pulled into the dump, Jim would welcome you personally and quiz you about the nature of your garbage. Depending on what you were dumping, he would guide you to the right spot in the dump to throw that stuff.

Jim examined every load of garbage with the eye of someone who has never had much money and doesn't like to see anything wasted.

"That lamp is too good to throw away!" Jim would say. Or, "I'll bet somebody could really use that canister for something."

When Jim spotted something that he thought too nice to throw, he would place it on display near the gate. As new folks showed up, Jim would point out his little lineup of treasures and invite the newcomers to take anything they thought they could use.

I sometimes took stuff to the dump when I didn't really need to. It was fun just to talk to Jim and find out what had been happening in the area. Jim was the single best source of information about how the fish were biting in the bay, where the best blueberries could be found and who had been dealing with a garbage-eating bear. Jim knew everything that had happened, and he loved to tell stories.

He's gone now, as is the dump. My little town now has a recycling center. The folks there don't know anything about fishing or bear attacks, and I never bother going.

The typical small-town cafe is not just a place to catch up on local gossip. The regulars there know where to buy firewood, who is the most dependable plumber, and which teenagers might agree to mow your lawn. You might even find a caretaker to tend your place while you're gone.

Locals are familiar with the animal pests. Their advice on how to deal with troublesome animals will usually be practical and effective.

When you need a local person with particular skills, that person can be hard to find using city methods (such as the Yellow Pages). Local residents are a treasure trove of information about which local workers are skillful and reasonable.

Even in popular vacation areas, there are often some secluded picnic spots, scenic walks or hidden beaches that are not well publicized. The local residents often know

about these spots. They won't talk about them to just anybody, but they might share this information if they conclude that you are a good person.

Vacation homeowners from metro areas, although highly successful in their fields, are usually amateurs at managing rural life. The vacation home presents them with unusual challenges in the form of damp basements, balky chain saws and critters that freely invade the garden. Local folks have a wealth of practical knowledge and are usually eager to share it with a respectful outsider who needs help.

The local residents know much that city folks don't know. Their area of special knowledge is priceless for owners of vacation land. Most of that information is free for the asking for those who know how to ask.

SMALL-TOWN SOCIETY

Outsiders are often confused by differences in communication styles between metro areas and small towns.

For a variety of reasons, people in small towns don't often use official sources of information, such as experts who might be associated with universities and governmental agencies. Often, they don't look up the answers to life's challenges on the Internet or in libraries.

Small-town folks live in a rich cultural network that depends on personal contact and conversation. Information in vacation land areas tends to be carried in the heads of local people. A metro person who needs information tries to get it by consulting some useful source. The local resident in vacation land is more likely to ponder his or her network, and then begin putting out inquiries. Pretty soon several other people will be actively involved in the quest for that information. Sooner or later, someone will remember the right person to ask.

Similarly, you shouldn't expect small-town folks to use the same communication technologies so popular in metro centers. Don't expect everyone to have a mobile phone or an answering machine. It wouldn't occur to my friend, Harold, to use an answer-

FINDING STEVE DENKER

Shortly after buying my cabin along the shores of Lake Superior, I decided that I needed the help of a carpenter. Everyone told me the right person to contact was Steve Denker, a young man who did good work and didn't charge too much.

When I tried to contact Steve, I met with one frustration after another. He wasn't home during the day for the obvious reason that he was off working on a job. He didn't have an answering machine. I tried calling him several times, and the only time I got an answer it turned out to be a small child who did not relay my message to Steve.

I finally realized I was behaving inappropriately for my small adopted community.

I walked into one of my town's two local taverns and hopped up on a stool. When the bar maid asked what I wanted, I told her, "I'll have a glass of Special Export. And what I really want is some way of contacting Steve Denker."

She narrowed her eyes for a moment as if I were pulling some joke on her. Then, with a quick nod of her head, she said, "Umm, Steve's on the stool next to you."

I needed to contact Steve again a little later in the summer. This time I went directly to the same tavern. Steve was on the same stool where I'd found him earlier, wearing what seemed to be the same clothes and drinking what seemed to be the same beer.

"You are easy to find," I said. "All I have to do is go to the nearest bar."

Steve smiled warmly and said, "Yup. And you're easy to find, too. All I have to do is go to the nearest bar and wait for you to come in!"

ing machine to catch calls at home when he is in his store. Nobody would be stupid enough to call Harold's home phone when he is at the store. Everyone—literally everyone who might want to talk to him—knows when Harold is at his store. Local people who want to speak to Harold during his store hours know enough to call the store. More likely, they jump in the pickup and drive to the store so they can chat with Harold in person, for that is a bit more personal and polite.

Conflict is usually handled differently in small towns or rural areas that are thinly settled. Conflict is personal and less legalistic in rural areas and small towns than it is in major cities. Outsiders who have disagreements with local residents might be tempted to call the authorities—the police, for example, or the local conservation officer—to resolve things. The folks who live in little villages or rural areas near vacation lands will not take that well. It is considered rude and inappropriate to bring officialdom into a personal dispute.

Usually, the best way to contact a person in such a small community is to ask someone if they've seen that person lately. You will do better if you ask a person who is positioned centrally to notice everyone else's comings and goings. Teenagers only keep track of other teens, so they aren't the best source of help. You'll do better by asking the guy who runs the gas station, the postmistress, the clerk at the general store.

Small-town people keep track of each other without even being aware of the fact they are doing it. Whatever they are doing, they are at least subliminally aware of the activities of others. When I needed to contact Jesse Kaseno, I asked the checkout clerk at the grocery store if she'd seen Jesse. She had. She said, "Well, I saw his white pickup going up the hill on C behind town, so he's

probably visiting his folks for a while. Otherwise, he's been doing a lot of work on the new cabin out on Spirit Point. You could check there."

SPENDING MONEY IN SMALL TOWNS

Outsiders can often sense that local residents in vacation areas regard their presence as a mixed blessing. On one hand, outsiders represent some degree of intrusion in the normal life of the area. But their dollars are vital to making the local community hum, and their presence adds interest to an area that is pretty sleepy and dull when nobody but the locals is around.

Local residents sometimes misjudge how wealthy outsiders are. They sometimes feel that everyone makes more money than they do, and sometimes locals tend to view summer people too much in terms of how much they might spend locally. But that is within your control when you enter a local community. If you deal with the locals as human beings who are interesting and worthy of your regard, they will not view you as a walking checkbook.

It is wise to patronize local shops whenever possible. If you are going to make a trip to your property, for example, you could go to a supermarket or discount store near home and stock up. You would find what you need, and the prices would be great. On the other hand, you could wait to shop for the same stuff locally when you arrive. If so, you might not find exactly the items you want, and you may pay a bit more for them.

It is a tradeoff. Buying locally helps you develop friends in the local community, friends who might later help you in ways you could never anticipate. As much as possible, I try to buy locally. I am not fond of blackened bananas or slimy lettuce, so I buy most of my produce from supermarkets before I leave home. But whenever I can, I buy staples and hardware and other goods in the village near my cabin. Buying locally supports my friends and feels better. Chatting with Helen at the cash register is more fun than saving a buck or two.

Similarly, it is smart to hire local handymen to do work for you. You'll generally find that they work hard, do superior work and charge perhaps half what workmen in metro areas would charge for the same project. Beyond that, hiring local people that way integrates you into the community to a degree. Local people have long memories for people who patronize their store or hire their services.

You can get some great bargains by hiring local handymen. The flow of work in small towns and rural areas is often unsteady. A good carpenter might be busier than he wants to be for ten months, only to fall on lean times for two months of the year. If you are known and liked by the local folks, you might get a call from Ed when his work is slow. He knows you have wanted a gazebo for years but have worried about the price. Ed might call you and offer to do the project for less than he usually charges. He needs to keep some kind of cash flow, so it is in his interest and yours to go ahead with the gazebo project at a bargain rate.

If you hire local handymen, don't be shocked to learn that there are two possible prices for their services. If you insist on writing them a check and getting an invoice for their services, the price might be higher than if you pay in cash. People struggling to make a living often have one official job for which they claim all income and pay taxes, but perhaps they have one or two jobs on the side that they regard as being outside the tax system. Handle that as you will.

SOMEONE TO WATCH OVER ME

If you own property that you rarely get to visit, it is wise to have someone that you trust to check on your place from time to time. Ideally, this would be a neighbor or at least someone who passes by the place fre-

If your vacation home sits vacant for extended periods, having someone to check up on things periodically is essential. In regions with harsh winters, this can be especially crucial.

KEEP OUT!

Near my cabin in northern Wisconsin there is a little white cabin that sat empty for several years. One day the "For Sale" sign came down and was replaced by a big notice that barked, "No Trespassing!" The new owners blocked the driveway with a pole gate, securing it with a silver padlock as big as a man's fist.

I knew that gesture of distrust would offend local people. Local folks often walked down that driveway to get at a nice place to have picnics by the lake. They could still walk around the big pole, but the symbolism was all wrong. The culture in this region emphasizes trust and sharing. Vacation property in this region is not protected by tight security devices so much as it is by the fact that people there are honest, and meanwhile everyone keeps a friendly eye on deserted houses just to be sure they are okay.

After two years, the ugly No Trespassing sign came down. The big padlock disappeared and the gate was swung back to the open position. It has remained there ever since.

I never heard how the new owners learned that they had done something inappropriate. Most likely, someone waited until a friendly occasion arose when it was possible to mention the barrier and politely say, "It's your place, of course. But, you know, that's not the way we do things around here."

quently. If you are liked by your neighbors, people will look after your place without being asked to. But if your property sits idle for months at a time, you might want to ask someone in particular to check on it to make sure the place is in good shape.

You might want to make a formal arrangement for someone to check on your place. In that case, you will want to supply them with keys, instructions and a contact list of numbers to call in case something is out of order.

When you ask a local resident for a favor, you should be prepared to do them a favor in return. Metro residents usually offer to pay for such favors, for money is the universal form of exchange in much of their lives. Local residents might be embarrassed by taking money for doing something so casual and friendly. They might be more comfortable if you offer to reward their favor by offering favors of your own, such as sharing produce from your garden. It isn't "wrong" to offer money for small favors of this sort, but much of the time you will make people more comfortable if you can find a graceful way of saying "thank you" that doesn't involve dollar signs.

Trespass

One of the touchiest issues related to owning recreational property is what access to your land you permit to local people. Local people might have a tradition of using the land that you have just acquired. When they hear there is a new owner, those folks will naturally be anxious because they fear you might exclude them from enjoying land whose availability means a lot to them. That means that other people might earnestly feel entitled to trespass on your land, based on a history of use. If you take a stiff, legalistic view that they are not welcome, the results can be nasty.

The most volatile clashes involve land that has been hunted for decades by a local group or family. If you do what seems the natural

Be sensitive to the hunting traditions in the area. Most hunters will respect your wishes if you'd rather they not hunt on your property. But you can also make good friends if you welcome responsible hunters.

thing to most folks by posting your property and trying to keep hunters out, you will acquire enemies. This kind of clash gets particularly ugly when it involves traditional areas to hunt deer. Local people have very strong feelings about land where they've grown up hunting deer. People coming into the area from metro regions can have equally strong opinions about people running around uninvited on their land, firing rifles. Be aware of the fact that your property might have a history of use by other folks and they will be threatened by what you mean to do.

There is no easy way to resolve such conflicts. If you feel the need to change historical patterns of use, do it as slowly and delicately as possible. A rigid, legalistic insistence on your rights will make you a set of local enemies, which is the last thing you need. If you can tolerate a certain amount of trespassing, do so. If you cannot, take your time when changing other people's use of your property. Network with local folks, finding out who actually uses your property. If you can, talk to them to show that you are a reasonable person. Do not bring the police or game wardens into the dispute.

A wiser approach is to try to persuade people to look for other places to hunt, taking several years to make your point. Don't threaten to have them arrested for violating your property rights; tell them that your kids are terrified by rifles. Go easy. Take your time. Let them get used to the fact that they aren't welcome on your land in the way they once were.

CHAPTER 7
GUESTS

ACCORDING TO THE OLD STEREOTYPE, WHEN YOU BUY A RECREATIONAL PROPERTY, YOU WILL SUDDENLY BE BESET WITH HORDES OF SHIRTTAIL RELATIVES AND CASUAL FRIENDS WHO DROP IN ON YOU TO TAKE ADVANTAGE OF FREE LODGING. AS THIS CLICHÉ GOES, SOME PEOPLE NEVER GET TO ENJOY THEIR COTTAGES BECAUSE THEY ARE WAITING ON SO MANY FREELOADERS.

That is hardly the problem with my cabin. Instead of an indoor toilet, I have an outhouse about twenty-five yards from the cabin, and that's a long way to trudge early in the morning when a chilly rain is falling. Since my cabin has no running water or shower, guests get a little ripe after two or three days in warm weather. I don't have a problem with unwelcome guests coming too often or staying too long.

Actually, I love entertaining guests. All joking aside, it isn't the lack of a shower or toilet that keeps people from visiting. Life is just too hectic these days. Vacation homeowners become accustomed to the rhythm of working a full week, driving several hundred miles on a Friday night and then returning home on Sunday. That schedule is brutal for most folks, however. Because of the pressures of the workplace, it is difficult for people to find enough free time to visit.

If you own a lovely spot in remote country, you will get visitors. People enjoy visiting, and hosting friends is a large part of the joy of owning a cottage in some wild and beautiful place. Depending on your property and your personality, you might even make the place available to guests when you cannot be present.

Entertaining guests is one of the fine arts of owning recreational property. There's a knack to doing it well.

Cabin rules

People who don't own vacation property have no idea how troublesome some simple things can be. For example, metro residents don't understand septic systems. I think of septic systems as being like senior citizens with digestive systems that are easily thrown off. At my cabin, garbage is a problem since the local recycling center has limited hours and too many fussy rules. We just hold garbage in the cabin and then take it home after a trip. Because of that, we avoid products with bulky packaging since we'll just have to transport that packaging back home. Little things like that can be important to someone living on recreational property.

You cannot expect your guests to know anything about these realities. It is up to you—the management—to educate your guests about the things you want your guests to do or not do. Many cottage owners use the phrase "cabin rules" for that. These rules don't have to be draconian or unpleasant—in fact it works to make a joke out of "cabin rules." Guests appreciate knowing what special expectations apply to them in this novel situation. The concept behind cabin rules is that this is a special place and there are special procedures that need to be followed.

Communicating your rules is a two-step process. The most important step is to let your guests know that certain realities require everyone to cooperate. The second step is to post clear instructions related to particular subjects, such as managing a woodstove or taking a shower.

You can post more detailed rules in appropriate places. Type up the instructions or rules and encase them in a plastic protector. Place one by the kitchen sink, one in the bathroom, one by the stove, one by the garbage and so forth.

Typical rules usually include the following:

• Please contribute to the overall effort of keeping things running properly. In other words, guests shouldn't expect to be served as if they were paying guests at a resort. Everyone can pitch in by vacuuming, washing dishes, stacking firewood or clearing brush. This will put many people at ease because they understand they are not free-loading.

• Do not flush anything you have not eaten first. This is especially important if you have a septic system, which can be disturbed or put out of balance by flushing harsh chemicals or pills.

• Keep showers brief. Again, this is especially important if you have a septic system, but typically necessary even if the place is served by a sewer system. Few vacation homes have enough bathrooms or hot water for guests to take 20-minute showers.

• Pets are (or are not) welcome. Guests might need to be instructed about protocols involving pets, particularly dogs. What kind of pet is welcome? Is it okay to let the family dog run in and out?

• Use fireplaces or woodstoves carefully. Since guests won't usually know how to run a woodstove, if you heat your cabin with wood you need to include careful instructions, including safety instructions. You will run the stove most of the time, of course, but you should have instructions to help your guests if they need a fire when you can't be around.

- Store all food securely. Guests may not be aware of the threats that mice and bears represent. Gently caution them against leaving food at ground level for mice, and instruct them to not store garbage anywhere bears might find it.

HOSTING WHEN YOU ARE GONE

Some owners share their vacation homes even if they can't be present. That takes trust, and not all properties are appropriate for this kind of sharing.

You probably want to hide a key in a safe place near the house. If guests go up without you, you can tell them where to find the key. Or you might divulge the location of the key so a tax assessor or repairperson can gain access when you can't be there. Someday you might forget to bring your own key, and then you'll be glad to have a spare key tucked away in a safe place.

Don't hide the key in an obvious spot. People predictably place spare keys close to the door (under the mat, in a flowerpot, on the lintel). Don't be that unimaginative. I also wouldn't have much faith in those phony rocks sold in mail-order catalogs that have key safes hidden on the bottom side, either. Those things are hardly a secret any more.

If you will be sharing your home, keys can be a problem. It helps to be a little more organized than most people usually are. Make at least one extra copy of each critical key, label the keys, and then store them in a safe place. Put prominent labels on the keys that you use most often.

Some families who own vacation property have learned it is handy to maintain a family web site. Free web sites are often included as part of the suite of services sold along with Internet access. Some innovative owners have created family sites with special pages devoted to the property. The web sites might include maps, driving instructions, cabin rules and photos of people having fun there. Guests can click their way to the web pages, download the driving instructions and learn about the area. The pages can include information that will help guests prepare for fun, such as telling them whether or not to bring a bathing suit and what kind of weather to expect.

Not everyone is quite that Internet-savvy. If you have a vacation home but don't have or care to use a web site like that, use old-fashioned technology to create good maps to your place, with instructions. You might try using one of the mapping web sites to come up with a good map. If you can click your way to the right map on the Internet, you will save a lot of time. Include appropriate contact phone numbers in case someone gets lost and needs help.

Guests will not know exactly how to get the place opened up and functional if you are not there to tell them. There should be a list that

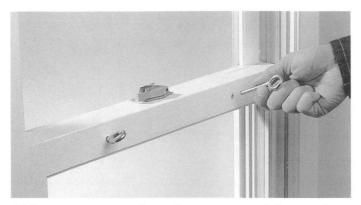

Make sure your guests know how to secure windows and doors before they leave your vacation home.

details the steps needed to unlock the place, get the power restored, turn on the propane tanks and generally get the place in good shape.

Some owners ask guests who stay two or three days on their own to make some small, appropriate contribution to upkeep. Propane, firewood and cooking staples aren't free. Guests who stay at my cabin often thank me by purchasing a fresh tank of propane or some firewood. You don't want your guests to feel they owe you the equivalent of a daily motel charge. On the other hand, inviting guests to help out a little can make them more comfortable about accepting your hospitality.

It doesn't hurt to remind guests to leave things in perfect order at the end of the trip. Leave instructions that include the locations of cleaning products. If you leave your refrigerator door propped open at the end of a visit, specify that; it wouldn't occur to most people otherwise.

Tell your guests exactly how to leave the place. There should be a specific, clear list of shutdown procedures. People who are not used to this lifestyle can easily forget that a window is open, which can lead to serious

problems if that window remains open for five weeks until the next time someone visits. People unaccustomed to rural life would probably not think to switch the power off at the circuit box and turn the propane off.

You should, of course, have a contacts list posted in a prominent place by the telephone. The most important thing to include is your various phone numbers. List the local police and fire numbers. The contact list should include the numbers for any friends and neighbors who might be useful if a problem arises.

SHUTDOWN PROCEDURES

We could put this discussion almost anywhere, but here—right after mention of unsupervised guests—seems as good a place as any. Every vacation home has certain shutdown issues, steps that should be taken to make sure the place will be secure and in good shape for the next visitor. And obviously enough, there will be issues of great concern for some homes that don't apply at all to others. This is a general guide. Our last chapter will include a more rigorous list of shutdown procedures for your last visit of the year.

First, the house needs to be thoroughly cleaned. Make a checklist of the important steps. Cleaning could take days if you let it, but if you bring organization and discipline to the process it should be possible to lash into the place vigorously for an hour and then be out the door.

Each vacation home has certain security issues that should be remembered when shutting down. That means closing and securing all windows, locking all doors and drawing curtains or drapes over windows so people looking in won't be tempted to break in by something they can see.

Leave everything in perfect order for the next person or group to use it. If you have been burning firewood and the stack of wood that is kept in an indoor rack has been depleted, refill it now.

If mice are an issue, bait traps or distribute poison dispensers as you leave. Place all food in mouse-proof containers and secure it against the insistent nibbling of mice.

Remove all perishable food. One of the nasty surprises people get upon arriving is the discovery that the last party left some perishable food in the fridge or elsewhere. All fruit, produce, milk, butter and other perishable food has to go back home unless the fridge will be left running until the next party arrives.

Wash out the fridge and prop the door open so mold and mildew do not form.

Leave on a light or two. It is courteous to turn on a light or two so that whoever arrives next won't have to walk into a dark cabin if they come past sundown. The light will go on when the circuit breaker is thrown on.

Replace the keys. If you have a key that needs to be hidden in its special place, remember it or the next person who needs it will be disappointed.

Turn off the power. Most owners feel it is safer to leave power turned off. If you have circuit breakers, snap them off as you go out.

SCRAMBLING HOME

The first time I stayed at the cabin of my friends, Bob and Eleanor, I was impressed by how low-keyed and effortless their hospitality was. Nobody worked hard at anything. Nobody hurried all weekend. We just relaxed and enjoyed the beauty of the cabin, an old log cabin structure that sat on a hill overlooking a lake famous for walleyes and loons that hooted wildly in the evening.

I was puzzled on Sunday morning because our hosts seemed unaware of the fact that we needed to pack up and head home before long. Still, the leisurely weekend went on. Bob quaffed coffee and read magazines. Eleanor puttered in the kitchen. The sweet relaxation of the weekend carried on until just past noon.

Eleanor said, "Well, Bob, should we?"

"Yeah," said Bob, "I guess we better."

And with that, the two slowest people in Hubbard County suddenly flew into action. Eleanor packed away food in the kitchen. Bob crated up the little TV that they'd brought from home. Our hosts barked out orders to us, their guests, about getting ready.

We hadn't seen Bob and Eleanor move quickly for three days, but now they seemed to fly through the steps needed to pack up and shut the cabin. Before I could believe it, we were in the car heading home. And I realized I had just learned my first important lesson in cabin living.

The lesson has several parts.

First, you should enjoy yourself while you are enjoying yourself. Make full use of cabin time to unwind and appreciate its special qualities. Don't, in other words, make the mistake of living in two places at once—your head at home while your body is at the cabin. Enjoy precious cabin time.

Second, I learned that tasks that could be unpleasant or difficult can be done almost instantly if you are practiced and organized. Bob and Eleanor, for all their apparent sloppiness, had a smooth routine that carried them through the nasty business of withdrawing from the cabin and packing for the inevitable return trip.

I learned that the key to enjoying cabin life without getting overwhelmed by its tasks is to use organization and discipline to limit the amount of time lost to the inevitable work side of making trips to the cabin.

Some cabins have a power box with a single lever that shuts off all electricity. In some cases you might want to leave a single circuit breaker or two on to power some implements (refrigerator, freezer, security light, dehumidifier, vent fan). If you have propane tanks, throttle them down tight.

FUN THINGS TO DO

Every recreational property should have a folder or organizer that is filled with information about fun things to do in that area. This can be stored in a convenient place where you can use it or guests can refer to it.

The folder should contain information about local businesses and their telephone numbers. It should have maps showing the way to local attractions. Many towns, counties or regions have free tourism brochures that are full of suggestions of places to go and contact information, and those obviously belong in the what-to-do folder. If there are local cruises or ferries, include a copy of their schedule and rates in the folder. Many regions rich in

A scrapbook showing fun activities to do in the area will be much appreciated by your guests.

vacation property have special publications that list all of the festivals, concerts, fairs and other special events of the summer.

You obviously can add your own typed up list of fun things to do. Make a list and add to it all the necessary information so your guests know where to go, when the attraction is available and whom to contact.

Consider creating a scrapbook of cabin photos. You can preserve your memories that way and create a showcase that shows your guests some of the fun things they can do in the area.

We have two additional traditions at my cabin that you might want to consider. We maintain a "cabin log" or diary of our cabin visits. It can be tedious to fill this out if you are running late and need to get back home. If you don't record your activities, they'll slip from memory, so I highly recommend the discipline of maintaining the log. Record your activities, any interesting conversations you had and any interesting wildlife sightings. You'll treasure this record later.

The other tradition is simpler and takes less discipline. I have a log book at the cabin that records all visitors. The rules on this are a little fuzzy, so if you visit a third and fourth time, I'm not sure if you are supposed to sign in each time. But I'm sure that each person who visits the cabin is required—absolutely required—to sign in on that first visit. This takes little time and makes for a nice little record of guests you have entertained over the years.

WELCOME TO OUR VACATION HOME

Your guests will need more detailed instructions on what to do when they arrive and when they leave. Use these lists as a starting point to make your own comprehensive lists.

When You Arrive

☐ Here's where to find the key.......
☐ Call to let us know you've arrived
☐ Open windows to ventilate
☐ Check for property damage
☐ Turn on furnace
☐ Open fireplace dampers
☐ Turn on water heater
☐ Check linens, change if necessary
☐ Inventory supplies on hand
☐ Sign log book
☐ _____
☐ _____
☐ _____

When You Leave

☐ Replace supplies you've used
☐ Mow lawn, water plants
☐ Change linens
☐ Clean bathroom, kitchen
☐ Replenish firewood supply
☐ Turn down/off furnace, water heater
☐ Shut all windows
☐ Call us to let us know you're leaving
☐ Lock doors
☐ Return key to hiding place
☐ _____
☐ _____
☐ _____

Helpful information

☐ Neighbor to contact in an emergency_____tel:_____
☐ Handyman_____tel:_____
☐ Plumber_____tel:_____
☐ Best grocery store_____
☐ Hardware store_____
☐ Medical clinic/hospital_____
☐ Drugstore_____
☐ Sporting goods store_____
☐ Chamber of commerce/tourist office_____
☐ State parks_____
☐ Movie theater_____
☐ Family restaurants_____
☐ Golf course_____
☐ Riding stable_____
☐ Best fishing spots_____

CHAPTER 8

SUMMERTIME MAINTENANCE

VACATION TIME, AND THE LIVING IS EASY. YOUR WORK ON OPENING WEEKEND SHOULD HAVE SET YOU UP FOR A REASONABLY CAREFREE SEASON. STILL, YOU CAN'T TOTALLY FORGET MAINTENANCE. ENJOY YOUR COTTAGE IN ITS LOVELY LOCATION, BUT TRY TO KEEP THINGS IN GOOD SHAPE.

MILDEW

In some parts of the country, houses with basements are given to mold and mildew problems. Muggy air is a fact of life in many regions, but if you keep windows open and run fans, the upstairs living areas will usually be livable.

Basements present problems. Their cooler air causes moisture to condense on walls, and that encourages the development of ugly mold and mildew. If mold and mildew were just unsightly, they would be a nuisance, but mold raises respiratory health concerns.

You can discourage trouble by simply being careful. Don't leave damp towels or wet bathing suits in the basement to add their moisture to

A solution of ordinary detergent, bleach and water is the best cleanser for mildew and mold.

SOLUTIONS FOR BRICK STAINS

Efflorescence: Use a stiff-bristled brush to scrub surface with water. Add household cleaning solution if accumulation is heavy.

Egg splatter: Dissolve oxalic acid crystals in water in a nonmetallic container. Brush onto stained surface.

Iron stains: Dissolve oxalic acid crystals in water. Brush onto stained surface.

Ivy: Cut (do not pull) vines away from the surface. Let remaining stems dry up, then scrub them off with a stiff-bristled brush and household cleaning solution.

Oil: Make a paste of mineral spirits and an inert material, such as sawdust. Spread onto stain and allow to dry.

Paint stains: Remove new paint with a solution of trisodium phosphate (TSP) and water. Old paint usually can be removed with heavy scrubbing or sandblasting.

Plant growth: Apply weed killer according to manufacturer's directions.

Smoke stains: Scrub surface with a household cleanser containing bleach, or with a mixture of ammonia and water.

the already damp air. Run damp clothes through the washing machine and drier (if you have them). Many cabins aren't so well equipped, but you can always wash things and hang them out to dry on a clothesline. Clotheslines are a wonderful old-fashioned technology that costs nothing, is energy-efficient and produces clothes that smell good.

Chronically wet basements need the aid of a dehumidifier. They come in a variety of sizes, and all modern models are equipped with controls that let you set the humidity level that triggers the unit to turn on.

If you need to run a dehumidifier when you are away, set it up with a power outlet on a separate circuit breaker. When you leave and shut the cabin down for a week or two, snap off all power except the circuit breaker for the dehumidifier. Dehumidifiers usually have collecting pans that can be adapted to take some sort of drain hose that you can use to direct the water into a basement drain. That way you can leave the dehumidifier

Mildew and other forms of mold are a common problem in vacation homes, since they are often left tightly closed up for long periods of time. One of your routine tasks should be cleaning mildew and ventilating to eliminate moisture.

running for weeks without supervision.

If you have to remove mildew from walls, wash them down with warm suds and a brush, and then wipe everything dry. Stubborn patches can be washed off with a mixture of one quart chlorine bleach and a tablespoon of liquid detergent mixed in nine quarts of water. Use this only in a well-ventilated basement. Never mix ammonia products with bleach.

CHIMNEY MAINTENANCE

Woodstoves emit volatile gases that can condense in the chimney as liquids that then dry to form a tar-like substance called creosote. Creosote builds up silently in chimneys much like plaque in human arteries, and you often don't know you've got creosote problems until you have a disaster. Creosote

INSPECTING THE FLUE & DAMPER

Soot and creosote deposits, bird nests, fallen bricks, and other obstructions can cause serious problems when you light the first fire of the season. To inspect the chimney, open the fireplace flue and peer up through it. You should be able to see a shaft of light from above. If the firebox is too small for a clear view, use a bright flashlight and a mirror for the inspection **(photo A)**. If the flue is blocked, have it professionally cleaned. You may save money by

doing the job yourself, but working on the chimney can be precarious, and few homeowners have the equipment to do a thorough chimney cleaning.

Once you know the flue is clear, make sure the damper seals tightly **(photo B)**. When the fireplace is in use, the damper helps control the draft—how fast air goes up the chimney—and determines the rate at which the fire burns. If left open when the fireplace is not in use, a

damper can cause 10 to 15 percent of a home's heat to escape. Test the lever or chain that controls the damper; you should be able to tell when the damper is open or closed all the way. If the damper doesn't open or close completely, open it as far as you can and clear the area around its edges on all sides with a stiff-bristled brush. Remove any debris that may have fallen from the chimney, and try closing the damper again.

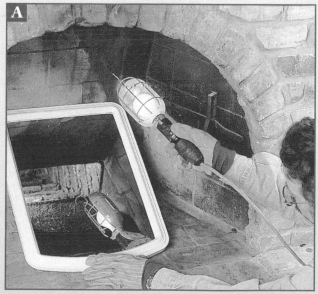

Use a mirror and a shop light to inspect the chimney easily from below.

Make sure the damper seals tightly, moves freely, and is free of dirt and debris.

TUCKPOINTING A BRICK CHIMMEY

Tuckpointing, the process of replacing failed mortar joints with fresh mortar, is the most common brick and block repair. Cracked or missing mortar not only makes a home look unkempt, it also invites moisture into a chimney structure, where it can cause additional damage. Tuckpointing techniques can be used to repair any structure where bricks or blocks are bonded with mortar.

Begin by using a mortar raking tool to clean out loose or deteriorated mortar to a depth of 1/4" to 3/4" **(photo A)**. Switch to a masonry chisel and hammer if the mortar is stubborn. Clean away all loose debris, then dampen the surface with water.

Mix the mortar, adding concrete fortifier and, if necessary, pigment to match existing mortar joints. Mix the mortar to a consistency that slides slowly off a trowel. Load the mortar onto a mortar hawk, then push the mortar into the horizontal joints with a joint filler **(photo B)**. Apply mortar in 1/4"-thick layers, allowing each layer to dry for 30 minutes before applying the next layer. Fill joints until the mortar is flush with the face of the brick.

Apply the first layer of mortar into the vertical joints by scooping mortar onto the back of a joint filler and pressing it into the joint **(photo C)**. Work from the top downward.

After the final layer of mortar is applied, smooth the joints with a jointing tool that matches the profile of the old mortar joints **(photo D)**, tooling the horizontal joints first. Brush off the excess mortar with a stiff-bristled brush. To slow down the drying time and strengthen the mortar's bond, periodically mist the repair area with water, or cover it with damp rags for several days.

Use a mortar raking tool to clean out loose or deteriorated mortar to a depth of 1/4" to 3/4".

Push mortar into the horizontal joints. Apply mortar in 1/4" layers until the mortar is flush with the face of the brick.

Scoop mortar onto the back of a joint filler and press it into the vertical joints. Work from the top downward.

Smooth the joints with a jointing tool. When mortar is dry, brush off the excess with a stiff-bristled brush.

is flammable. If there is enough creosote and the stove produces the right kind of heat, you can experience a full chimney fire. That is, the inside of your chimney can catch fire.

Chimney fires are frightening and destructive. In a chimney fire, the chimney roars like a runaway train and flames shoot out the top of the chimney well past the cap. Heat builds up around the chimney, with temperatures of 2,000 degrees F being possible. If your place has an old or poorly designed chimney, a chimney fire can set fire to the roof or walls. You are lucky if a chimney fire only destroys the chimney and doesn't also damage the rest of the building.

Several conditions exacerbate the buildup of creosote. One is burning slow, low-heat fires. Since the gases escaping from a smoldering fire don't rise with much heat, they are more likely to condense and adhere to the chimney. You increase creosote deposition if you burn wet firewood ("wet" meaning insufficiently seasoned). If your chimney was badly designed so that it tends to get cool, that will contribute to creosote buildup.

Prevention is obviously worth more than any kind of cure. Once each year, get up on a ladder and inspect your chimney. If there is a discernible layer of creosote near the chimney cap, call in a chimney sweep. Local residents will be able to tell you who will clean out your chimney for a reasonable price. You can do it yourself if you buy the right type of brush, but this is a messy job that is probably best done by a professional.

Most authorities say you should have your chimney swept once a year. That may be an excessive level of concern for recreational homes used mostly in summer. Unless you burn a lot of slow, smoldering fires, you are safe if you check your chimney yourself once a year and have a professional clean you out when it seems necessary.

Any time you check for creosote, remember to replace the cap on your chimney. Bats and raccoons often enter cabins via uncapped chimneys.

If you get a chimney fire, the best thing to do is call for help and run for safety. You can sometimes slow down a chimney fire by throttling off the air supply at the stove. Sprinkling water on the roof or walls near the chimney might help a little. But by the time you have a chimney fire you are already in deep trouble and should mainly be concerned with getting all humans and pets to safety until the fire department arrives.

WELLS

Many vacation homes get their water from private wells. Wells, if properly built, need little maintenance.

If you have an old well or plumbing that might include lead pipes, consider replacing them because water standing in a lead pipe can become contaminated (and cabin water often stands a long time when vacation property is not being used). You can reduce the threat of lead poisoning by running the water until the water is colder, which indicates that it is fresh.

Well water should be tested from time to time. Some authorities suggest doing this once a year. If your water has tested safe year after year, you might feel safe letting it go longer than that. You want to be careful about water quality if you have a septic system, as that increases the chances for contamination of your water supply.

Contact your local health department for details on testing. Some states issue kits that you use to take a sample that you then mail to a laboratory. A charge of about $25 is typical. You should test again any time your water becomes smelly or has an "off" flavor.

MAINTAINING WATER PUMP SYSTEMS

If you have low pressure problems with your well system, you may simply need to adjust the pressure setting on your pump.

Your pump's maximum pressure rating should be listed near the gauge, but it may also be in your owner's manual. If you can't locate the maximum ratings for your pump, contact the manufacturer.

If your pump's maximum setting is higher than the current setting, adjustments are easy.

Turn off the power to the pump and remove the cover on the pressure switch to access the adjusting

nut on the tall spring (**photo C**).

Raise the pressure incrementally by turning the nut clockwise—one-and-a-half turns raises the pressure by about 3 pounds. Cover the pressure switch and turn on the power. To make sure your adjustments have not increased the pressure above the maximum rating, watch the gauge as the pump runs through an entire cycle.

If the pump starts and stops frequently, the tank may be waterlogged. To correct this, drain the tank and allow it to fill with air passively.

First, close the supply valve

between the pump and the water tank (**photo D**). Turn on a cold-water faucet in the house to prevent a vacuum in the piping system.

Open the drain valve near the tank and allow the tank to drain completely. Wait a few minutes, then turn off the house faucet and close the drain valve.

Open the valve between the pump and the tank. As the tank fills, the water will pressurize the air cushion.

If this doesn't solve the problem, the pressure switch or air volume control may need to be serviced by an expert.

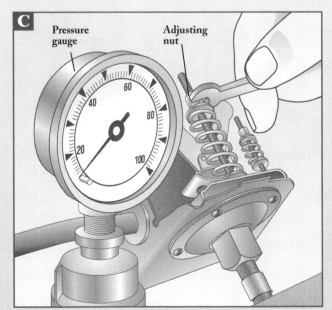

Tighten or loosen the adjusting nut in small increments to increase or decrease the pressure in the tank.

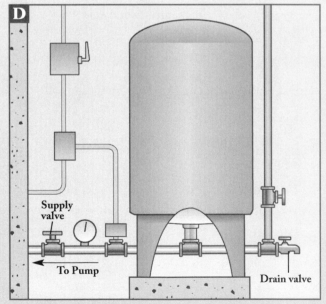

A waterlogged tank can be fixed by shutting the supply valve, opening the drain valve, and running cold water in the house while the tank fills with air.

MAINTAINING YOUR SEPTIC SYSTEM

Have your tank inspected and emptied regularly.	A neglected tank will cause your system to fail, resulting in sewage backup and posing a serious risk to your family's health.
	Experts recommend pumping a septic tank every one to two years.
Avoid using chemicals.	Harsh chemicals and antibacterial agents kill the bacteria your system depends on.
	Keep these chemicals out of your toilets and house drains:
	Drain cleaner
	Paint and paint thinner
	Chemical cleaners
	Chlorine – including toilet bowl flush-cleaners
	Antibacterial soft-soaps
Limit kitchen wastes.	Grease and fat from food hinder the septic process by coating drain pipes, interfering with bacterial breakdown in the tank, and clogging the loose-fill material in the drain field.
	Food disposers overload your system with solid food particles, sometimes doubling the rate of sludge accumulation in the tank.
	Throw cooking grease and food scraps in the garbage or compost heap.

Limit water inflow.
  Repair leaky plumbing fixtures as soon as possible.
  Route roof drains out of the house drain system.
  Don't drain a swimming pool or hot tub into the house drain.
	Excess water speeds up the flow through the septic system. The natural bacteria can't do its job, allowing too many solids to pass into the drain field.

Never use additives.	Biological additives designed to stimulate bacterial growth often harm more than they help. These additives agitate the anaerobic bacteria in the septic tank, and the increased activity forces undissolved solids into the drain field.

Wells can get contaminated, and that is a matter for professionals to handle. In most cases, water that acquires a strange taste is perfectly safe to drink, but you want to be sure. It is sometimes possible to purify a contaminated well through "shock chlorination." The most common source of well contamination in many parts of the country is agricultural chemicals. Fortunately, they aren't commonly found at high levels in most vacation country.

For your peace of mind, you might want to install a filter system. The most expensive is a "whole house" system. You can install an "under sink" filter system on just the kitchen sink. Even less expensive is a small system that fits under the sink and has a separate spigot and control. You would use water from this spigot only for drinking or cooking.

Septic systems

Septic systems, like wells, don't need much maintenance if they are built properly to begin with. The proper installation starts with careful soil sampling of the system. There are also concerns about how close a septic system can be located with respect to other objects, primarily your well and any water feature, such as a lake or stream. State health departments list explicit guidelines for such issues.

Old vacation properties often have badly designed septic systems that are located too close to water frontage. If that might be true of yours, check with your county government to request an inspection. You won't enjoy the expense of putting in a new septic system, and yet you surely don't want to live with the idea that your waste is polluting the water you love.

Septic systems involve a big holding tank that is designed to let solids settle out. After the solids have dropped away, the water is spread in the soil where evaporation and natural bacterial action purifies it. Nutrients are absorbed by plant life and microscopic organisms break down remaining biological contaminants.

Assuming your septic system was designed and built properly, you shouldn't have to do much in the way of maintenance. Strictly avoid commercial additives that claim to help or cure septic system problems. They are more likely to cause than to solve problems. Authorities claim that the only chemicals that might have a positive impact on a septic system are not sold to private individuals. You know you have trouble with your septic system if you experience sewage backup in the drains or toilets, slow flushing, wetness around the drain field or unpleasant odors.

Basic maintenance involves having your system inspected and pumped out on a regular basis. Never let the system go more than three years between pumping, and annual pumping might improve how well your system works. Pumping out your system costs far less than replacing a failed system. Have your system pumped by a competent professional who will do all the necessary inspections. Don't let anyone pump your system out through the inspection port. Only hire licensed professionals to pump your system.

SEPTIC SYSTEMS

Once problems arise within a septic system, there isn't much a homeowner can do, but being able to identify signs of trouble may prolong the life of your system and will probably save you some money.

If your drains are working slowly, or not draining at all, there may be a clog in the main house drain, or the septic system may be backed up. Check for clogs first. Use a motorized auger (photo, right) to clear the main drain. Never use chemical drain cleaners.

If the house drain isn't clogged, the problem may be a clogged drain field, an absence of bacteria in the system, or a full septic tank.

In addition to slow drainage, common signs of trouble include the presence of dark-colored water on the surface of the drain field and a sewage odor in or around the home.

Any of these symptoms may indicate a serious problem. Human sewage is considered a hazardous waste, and there are strict regulations governing its removal. Servicing a septic system isn't something you should try to do yourself.

Septic tanks produce explosive methane gas and may contain deadly viruses. Contact a licensed sewer service to have your septic system inspected and serviced.

If your system is sick and needs help, hire a licensed and bonded professional to restore it to health.

One simple rule for keeping a septic system running in good health is to limit water usage. Limit showers to ten minutes. Consider switching old toilets to modern models that use little water to flush. Conserve dishwater and laundry use by only running them when needed and only with a full load. Above all, don't allow your toilet or sinks to develop leaks. A running toilet uses far more water than you would guess.

Don't put things into the septic system that are likely to give it trouble. Bag garbage rather than using a disposal, and never put coffee grounds down the drain. Never dump chemicals, paints, cleaners or medicines down the drain. These can kill the helpful bacteria. Minimize the amount of toilet paper that goes into the system, and use paper that dissolves readily (you can test this). Use low-phosphate, liquid laundry detergent. Use as little bleach as possible. Consider installing a filter on your washing machine and buying a washing machine with a suds-saver device that recycles water.

FIREWOOD

It is smart to renew your supply of firewood in spring or early summer. You want a good supply of wood drying throughout the summer. "Green" firewood is hard to burn and will deposit more creosote than dry wood. Cut or buy your wood as early in the season as possible. There is some variation based on the type of wood involved, but most wood types will be dry after four months of exposure to the air. Wood that you split and stack in May will be dry and ready to burn in October.

FIRE IN THE WOODS

Americans living in modern metro areas have lost the fear of fire that haunted earlier generations of Americans. The most dangerous times of all were those decades right after loggers had removed all the towering pines. After an area was logged the forest floor was littered with branches and woody debris that was extremely flammable. Fires were one of the most terrifying facts of existence for pioneers. Forest fires were frequent, and they were deadly.

Fire is much less of a concern for people living in modern homes. Building codes and manufacturing standards have greatly reduced the risk of fire, although fires still happen and still can be fatal. Smoke alarms and the presence of professional fire departments further minimize the risk of home fires.

Those reassurances don't necessarily apply to cabins and cottages. Cabins are rarely built "to code" with all the modern safety considerations. Houses that are heated with wood face a much greater risk of fire. There are some very specific specifications applying to safe stove and chimney installations. Never, ever guess or take shortcuts with the installation of a woodstove or its chimney. Install smoke alarms (preferably hard-wired, not battery operated) and at least two good fire extinguishers.

You don't want to count on much help from the local fire department if your home is in a lightly settled vacation area. Tiny towns in vacation areas might not even have a fire truck. If they've got one, it might be a reject from a "real" fire department, and the fire department will probably be staffed by volunteers.

A friend who lives near my northern Wisconsin cabin had a fire erupt in a pole barn he had just built behind his home. John erected this large pole barn to house a collection of boats. His plan was to pay for the barn with the rental fees he charged for protecting the boats over the winter. John had just taken in his first collection of boats, about eight beauties of various sizes. He hadn't gotten around to buying insurance for all of this.

John told me, "Sometime in the middle of the afternoon, I smelled smoke. When I looked out my kitchen window I saw smoke boiling out from under the eaves of the pole barn. So I called the fire department."

"How did that turn out, John?"

"Well, there wasn't nobody around. Nobody! So they ended up doing the usual. They ran to the bars and collected as many guys as they could find. Of course, you get a bunch of geezers with nothing better to do in the middle of the afternoon but drinking—well, they're not going to be world-class firemen! When that crew finally got here, there wasn't anything left to do but just watch all those boats burn!"

You usually have a choice of buying firewood split or whole, and split firewood is always more expensive since you are paying someone else to do that work. If you have to split your own, use a splitting maul, not an axe. The right splitting maul will have a fat face that forces wood open. Mauls are heavier than axes, which helps you deliver enough force to split the wood. Don't use a maul that is too heavy for you to swing with authority. A six-pound maul is best for most users, as weight is much less important than head speed. Mauls with fiberglass handles are far superior to those with wood handles. It is important to use a chopping block that positions your firewood up above ground level. If you are faced with a really difficult load of wood that keeps trapping your maul, you might want the aid of special wedges sold for this purpose.

A firewood shed and chopping block are fixtures for many vacation homes. Firewood shelters can be purchased in kit form, or you can build your own following the plan on page 130.

If you have a lot of wood to split, you might want to rent a splitter. These have an engine that drives a blade through the stick of wood. People who make a living selling firewood know how to use these to good advantage. The folks I know who have rented splitters have often decided that it was just as much work to feed logs to the splitter as it is to whale away with a splitting maul.

Stack firewood in a single row. Inexpensive cribs and framing devices can make this easier. Place firewood stacks a good distance from all buildings so you don't attract critters that then might try to get inside. The ends of the firewood sticks should be exposed to as much sun and wind as possible for fast drying. If you build a stack near a woodshed, for example, don't jam the ends of the logs right against the sides of the shed. If you leave a bit of a gap, the air can circulate better around both ends of the wood pieces. You can cover the top of the stack. Don't cover the stick ends.

Most people know that different woods have different burning characteristics. In general, hardwoods outperform softwoods. They catch fire more easily, burn longer and put out more heat. The hardwoods most often used for cabin heat are oak and the many different types of maple. Birch is not really a hardwood, but it burns well. Aspen is less desirable, and the worst species of all are spruce and fir.

CHAPTER 9

SHORELINE AND LAWN MAINTENANCE

S EVERAL YEARS AGO I RETURNED TO THE
MINNESOTA LAKE WHERE OUR FAMILY USED TO
TAKE VACATIONS IN THE LATE 1950S. IT HAD
BEEN CLOSE TO FIFTY YEARS SINCE I'D SEEN IT.

The lake was so drastically changed that I could hardly bear to look
at it. Quaint old cabins have been leveled and replaced with squat
modern mansions. A wonderful old stump bay, full of lily pads and
turtles, had been cleared out. Long stretches of forest and native shoreline vegetation were gone. Gone were the lovely birches and the red
pines that had perfumed the breezes with their tangy scent. They had
been replaced by manicured lawns, one after the other, with vast bor-
ing acres of Kentucky bluegrass and some plastic lawn furniture. What
had been a beautiful lake looked like a suburb with a water feature.
Not coincidentally, the fishing was terrible. I went home two days
early, even though I had paid for a week at the resort.

Unfortunately, what happened to that lake is happening all over
vacation land in state after state. Natural shoreline is being replaced by

"Natural lakescaping" is the phrase used to define the practice of leaving shoreline areas to native plants rather than creating manicured lawns. Such practices create wildlife habitat, and reduce harmful runoff of fertilizers and pesticides into lakes, marshes and streams.

green turf lawns. That is causing shorelines to erode and wash away. That, in turn, degrades water quality and destroys the aquatic vegetation in the lake that is home to fish populations.

The way most people think they "should" manage lakeshore lawns is harmful to wildlife, fish and lakes. To most people who own lakeshore, a highly manicured green lawn looks neat and well tended. People also favor flat lawns because level lawns maximize views of the lake. The ideal is a flat stretch of bluegrass that terminates at the lake, with maybe a bit of sandy beach for swimming. Instead of seeing aquatic and shoreline vegetation as a natural element of the lake ecosystem, lakeshore owners see these as undesirable weeds, and they eliminate these wonderful plants.

Sometimes the greatest ecological damage is done not by rapacious polluting industry but by hundreds of thousands of people who, with the best of intentions, manage their lands in ways that destroy natural values. The sterile, closely-cropped look of a lawn seems attractive to only one wildlife species. Geese like to graze on grassy lawns, and they reward the homeowner with liberal deposits of goose poop.

My Wisconsin cabin could not be more different. The original owner vigorously advocated for keeping native vegetation intact. He used to lecture his neighbors about the virtues of maintaining lakeside lands as naturally as possible. He decided to sell to me when I told him I wouldn't take a lawn mower anywhere near the property. I remember telling him that if a lawnmower did manage to sneak onto my property, I would shoot it on sight.

My cabin's front area is more of a forest than a lawn. The land has so many trees and shrubs that deer feel perfectly secure as they pass through the land between the cabin and the lake. I've cut lanes in the brush so people sitting in key spots in the cabin have good views of the lake. But from the lake, my cabin is invisible behind all the trees and shrubbery, even in winter. There are people who have fished in front of my place for years without knowing there was a cabin hiding behind that wild, natural piece of shoreline.

There is now a strong movement coming from state departments of natural resources, watershed districts and extension divisions. The phrase "natural lakescaping" suggests the basic idea behind the new thinking. Some landowners are now leaving more natural vegetation shoreline intact, and a few landowners are now paying to restore natural vegetation along shores and on their lawns in an effort to improve the lakes they love.

Natural landscaping and lakescaping are attractive ideas to cabin owners who aren't absolutely committed to the ideal of the manicured lawn. The natural alternative costs less to maintain. People spend a lot to put chemicals on their lawns, and then they burn expensive gas to mow those lawns. Moreover, maintaining a closely cropped lawn takes a great deal of time. The time spent mowing lawns could be spent fishing, hiking or swimming. The natural alternative is kinder on the environment, easier on your wallet and gives you more time to enjoy your vacation home.

CONVENTIONAL LAWN EFFECTS

Managing lakeshore lawns in the conventional way is bad for lakes in several ways.

Because turf grass has short roots (usually less than three inches), it cannot stabilize soil as well as native plants such as switch grass (with roots three to five feet deep). Soil washes into the lake during storms, which reduces water quality, degrades the shoreline and destroys the aquatic vegetation that is essential fish habitat.

Conventional lawns have no way to hold water during a rainstorm. Water rushes off the land into the lake at high speed, eroding the topsoil and depositing salt, herbicides and fertilizer in the lake. The speed of water flowing off the lawn into the lake then breaks down the shoreline and destroys vegetation.

Conventional lawn management uses chemicals that harm water quality, especially the phosphorous in fertilizer. This leads to algae blooms.

Unhealthy runoff and pollution harm the desirable aquatic plants in the lake, inviting the growth of nuisance weeds while depriving fish and wildlife of the benefit of the natural vegetation. As the natural aquatic vegetation dies, the wave action strikes the shoreline with more force, hastening the degradation of the shoreline. That ultimately hurts fish populations and favors rough fish like carp instead of bass, walleyes or muskies.

LOOSE-FILL PATHWAY

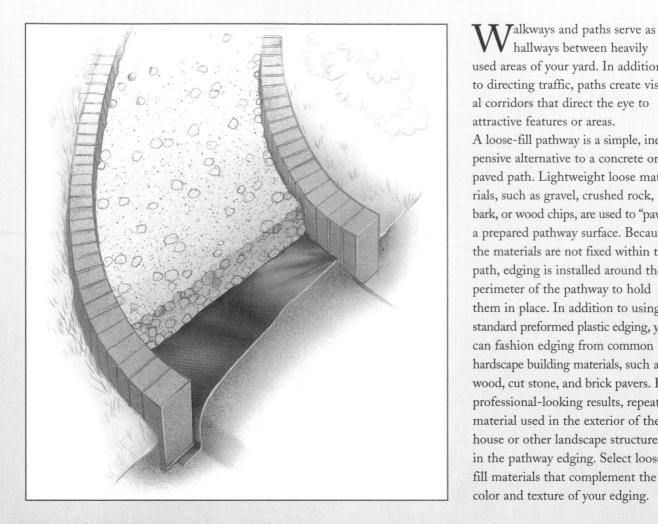

Walkways and paths serve as hallways between heavily used areas of your yard. In addition to directing traffic, paths create visual corridors that direct the eye to attractive features or areas.

A loose-fill pathway is a simple, inexpensive alternative to a concrete or paved path. Lightweight loose materials, such as gravel, crushed rock, bark, or wood chips, are used to "pave" a prepared pathway surface. Because the materials are not fixed within the path, edging is installed around the perimeter of the pathway to hold them in place. In addition to using standard preformed plastic edging, you can fashion edging from common hardscape building materials, such as wood, cut stone, and brick pavers. For professional-looking results, repeat a material used in the exterior of the house or other landscape structures in the pathway edging. Select loose-fill materials that complement the color and texture of your edging.

Dig narrow trenches for the edging on both sides of the excavated path site. Check the depth with a brick paver.

Place strips of landscape fabric over the path and into the edging trenches, overlapping sections by 6".

Our loose-fill project uses brick edging set in soil, which works well for casual, lightly traveled pathways. However, this method should be used only in dense, well-drained soil. Bricks set in loose or swampy soil won't hold their position.

Loose-fill materials are available at most home and garden stores. Many stores sell these materials prebagged, which makes transporting and applying them easier. Aggregate supply companies also sell crushed rock and pea gravel in bulk, which is often a less expensive option. If you buy loose-fill material in bulk, it may be easier to have the supplier deliver it than to transport it yourself.

As you prepare to build a path, consider how it will normally be used, keeping in mind that loose-fill pathways are best suited to light-traffic areas. Also think about how the path will fit into the overall style an shape of your landscape. Curved pathways create a soft, relaxed look that comple-ments traditional landscape designs, while straight or angular paths fit well in contemporary designs. You may want to strategically place the path to lend depth to an area or highlight an interesting element.

HOW TO CREATE A LOOSE-FILL PATHWAY

Step A: Excavate the Path

1. Lay out the shape of the path with a rope or garden hose, then use a spade to excavate the area to a depth of 3". Rake the site smooth.

2. Dig narrow edging trenches along both edges of the path site, using a trenching spade or hoe. Make the trenches about 2" deeper than the path.

3. Test the trench depth with a brick paver placed on end in the trench—the top of the brick should stand several inches above ground. If necessary, adjust the trench to bring the bricks to the correct height.

Step B: Add Landscape Fabric

Line the trench with strips of land-scape fabric, overlapping the strips by at least 6". Push the ends of the landscape fabric into the edging trenches.

Step C: Set the Bricks

1. Set the bricks into the edging trenches. Arrange them side by side, with no gaps between bricks.

2. Using a trowel, pack soil behind and beneath each brick. Adjust bricks as necessary to keep rows even.

Step D: Spread the Loose-fill Material

1. Spread the loose-fill material, adding material until it sits slightly above ground level. Level the surface, using a garden rake.

2. Tap the bricks lightly on the inside faces to help set them into the soil. Inspect and adjust the bricks yearly, adding new loose-fill material as necessary.

Install bricks end to end and flush against each other in the trenches, then pack soil behind and beneath each brick.

Fill the pathways with loose-fill material. Tap the inside face of each brick paver with a mallet to help set them permanently in the ground.

Natural settings are one of the charms of vacation home life. They also reduce maintenance chores, leaving more time for recreation.

NATURAL LAKESCAPING

The new standard of beauty represented by the phrase "natural lakescaping" will not be acceptable to everyone, and certainly there is a large need for education so more owners of recreational lands understand all the negative consequences of managing lakeshore like city lawns. Because there can be issues with neighbors, it is wise for anyone interested in switching to natural lawn and shoreline management to work through a community association. A few well-informed opinion leaders can accomplish a lot that way.

The first step toward moving to new management is often to create or contact a community association and begin a dialogue. If you want to open a discussion of the issue you will find a great deal of help available. There is no shortage of educational materials for you. State, county and local managers will be eager to cooperate by helping to promote and plan the transition to ecologically friendly management practices. Depending on what state you live in, your local hydrologist or lake management agency will have educational materials such as videos, pamphlets, CD-ROM disks or books. Contact your local water conservation districts to see if they have a liaison person available to explain and help plan a switch to more ecologically sensitive management.

Your project will often start by excluding invasive vegetation. Purple loosestrife and Eurasian watermilfoil are two pesky aquatic invaders. You'll want to get rid of any invasive land species, such as reed canary grass and buckthorn, too. Native plants have evolved to function in this specific environment, making them the most attractive and effective choice for the people who want to protect the lake.

You don't need to think in terms of letting your whole lawn revert to woods. Patches of native vegetation interspersed with mowed lawn are far healthier than vast unbroken stretches of manicured lawn. Consider such landscaping measures as putting in meandering paths or setting up terraces—anything that discourages water from rushing straight down the lawn unhindered and into the water.

Some owners divide their lawns and devote half of them to oval stands of natural vegetation that stand like small gardens. This works best if you alternate patches of native vegetation with patches of lawn, so that your lawn has pockets of lush vegetation scattered around to catch runoff. What you do not want is a lawn that allows water to get a straight, unbroken downhill run over grass.

If you own waterfront property, the most important step in conservation is to set up a buffer or "filter strip" at the lakeshore. You want a variety of natural vegetation species growing in the water and at the water's edge to stabilize the banks and filter out pollutants washing off the lawn. With a good buffer strip on the shoreline, you can have a lot of turf lawn and still minimize the damage done to the lake.

This kind of management is compatible with having a dock and swimming area, although you should try to minimize the impact of the developed area of shoreline. In other words, instead of having a hundred feet of swimming beach, settle for a small swimming area right around the dock and let the rest of the

An ordinary bow saw is one of the best tools for clearing brush and small trees from your property.

shore return to natural shoreline vegetation. Native vegetation on your land helps preserve healthy aquatic vegetation in front of your property. That vegetation, in turn, helps damp out the effects of waves so that you don't lose more shoreline. If you cut or pull the native vegetation in front of your property to make a swimming area, wave action will become harsher and will tend to wash out even more vegetation than you wanted to get rid of.

If you cannot make this transition to natural lakescaping and are losing shoreline, consider the expensive step of installing rock rip-rap. This usually requires a permit, and it is not a step you should take lightly. Natural lakescaping is less expensive and kinder on the lake, but a good rip-rap installation is better than letting your lawn wash away into the lake.

If you maintain a conventional lawn, be extremely careful about introducing pollutants. Your septic system should not be too close to the lake, and you need to have it pumped out and maintained so it functions well. Some states now flatly forbid the use of phosphorous fertilizer on lakeshore lawns. Any fertilizer whose packaging has a number with a zero in the middle has phosphorous. An example would be "22-0-15" fertilizer. That zero means it carries phosphorous and is a threat to water quality.

If you cannot make the switch to natural lakescaping with a buffer strip of natural vegetation to filter and protect the shore, consider building up a berm along the shoreline. This is a slightly high "bump" of rock, soil and vegetation that holds water back so it doesn't rush off your lawn into the lake. The condition you most want to avoid is the one most lakeshore owners favor: a perfectly flat lawn that ends abruptly at the lake's edge.

TREES

Many recreational properties have mature trees on them. You cannot take the continued existence of trees for granted. Trees come and go, and you might need to replace them.

Small trees and brush can quickly overwhelm your property. To remove small trees, remove all the lower branches you can reach, then drop the tree with the aid of a helper.

It is smart to take photos of your property to record the amount of tree cover you have, for that will give you a baseline for knowing if you are losing or gaining tree cover.

Part of Opening Weekend should be doing an inventory of trees. They often come down in winter storms, although trees can be blown down, struck by lightning or killed by porcupines at many other times of year. Trees often don't fall all the way, getting hung up partway down by other trees. They are an obvious hazard. Get out your chain saw or hire a local helper to drop any hung trees. And be careful! If you aren't practiced in dropping trees, this is a job better left to someone who uses a chain saw every day.

Late in winter is the ideal time to look for potential trouble with limbs that seem weak or are extending out over the cabin or outbuildings. Prune aggressively to remove limbs that are a threat to your cabin or which seem to be dying. Removing lower branches can encourage a young tree to raise its crown. Consider hiring a professional to prune adult trees for their own benefit or to allow more sunlight to filter through.

Most cottage owners will want to do something with trees that have fallen and are on the ground. Chain saws make quick work of this task. You can limb the tree and cut it into sections. If it is a birch, oak or other good firewood species, you will probably want to move the sections to where you can split them and build a stack of firewood. Trash trees like black spruces should be sectioned up into small pieces for disposal.

My practice is somewhat unconventional but natural and inexpensive. I simply cut up and lop the limbs off downed trees. Then I let them decay where they fall. This, after all, is what happens in a forest. In that sense it is the most natural way of handling the downed trees. Old, dead trees break down and return their nutrients to the soil so younger trees and other types of vegetation can use them. If a downed tree is an absolute eyesore, I'll move the sections to places where they don't look bad, but on my brushy land the pieces are usually out of sight wherever they land. The point of cutting up a downed tree is to encourage the maximum amount of contact between the tree and the ground, which speeds up the process by which the wood breaks down and returns its nutrients to the soil.

If you count on natural reforestation to replace lost trees, you'll probably be disappointed. You might not get enough trees that way to keep up with your losses. The volunteer replacement trees might be an undesirable species or they might grow in an undesirable location. For all of these reasons, it is usually smart to maintain a steady practice of planting young trees.

In these days, planting young trees is just a way of feeding the deer unless you take measures to protect the tree from the ubiquitous whitetail. Drive stakes into the ground on two or three sides of a young tree and then wrap a blanket of metal mesh hardware cloth around the whole. Bury the protection two to three inches below ground level if there are many rodents that might attack a young tree. For deer, you need to protect the sapling to a height of about two feet above the level of the anticipated snow depth. So if your area gets about six inches of snow, the hardware cloth protection needs to cover the tree to a height of about three feet.

Lay down a base of mulch around the base of the trees you plant. A slow-release, nitrogen-based fertilizer will reduce winter stress and help plants recover vigorously in spring. Do not use too much fertilizer.

Planted evergreens are subject to winter stress. If exposed to too much wind and sunlight, young evergreens "blister" and turn brown because of excessive loss of moisture. It helps to plant evergreens in clumps so one tree helps to shelter others. You can also help protect a young evergreen with a sort of burlap fence in the shape of an "L" so it protects two sides of the young tree. Position the fence to offer protection against the worst wind and sunlight. Your extension division or local department of natural resources forestry office will have pamphlets to guide you.

MANAGING FOR FIRE SAFETY

In many states in the Southwest and West, tree and brush management is dictated by concerns about wildfires. Fires are much more of a threat to vacation property than they were in earlier times. There are far more roads crisscrossing wooded and mountainous country, with far more homes scattered along them in what once was solid woods. A fire that might have burned harmlessly in the past is likely to threaten property now because

there are so many more vacation properties deep in mountains and forests.

Wildfire is much more dangerous in the mountains of the West and Southwest than elsewhere in vacation areas. The air is much drier, so trees, shrubs and grasses are much more likely to be dry and flammable. The steep pitch of mountainous terrain encourages fires to spread uphill far faster than they can move along on level ground. A wildfire can occur in vacation areas almost anywhere in the nation, and yet fire is a dominating concern with cabins in the West.

The basic formula for safety is to set up a "defensible zone" around your property. That is, you need to clear a zone between the nearest fuel and your cabin. This is usually accomplished with three zones. Right under and next to the cabin you should have nothing flammable at all, not even grass. Or if you have grass, it should be short-cropped and watered so frequently it will not burn. This first circle should stretch from your cabin to about three feet.

The key zone is a thirty-foot circle around your cabin. This should have no fuel in the form of high grass, brush or shrubs. Any trees in this zone should have all branches removed up to a height of six to ten feet. Trees need to be spaced generously so that the edges of the crown are ten to sixteen feet apart. Allow nothing on the ground in this zone that could be fuel for a wildfire. A stone or brick wall or garden makes a good additional barrier if it is in this zone. Anything that breaks up a continuous stretch of grass or other fuel is a good idea here. You want fire breaks in this zone.

The third zone, the area beyond the outer limits of the second zone, can have deciduous trees and shrubs but should be thinned and pruned so there is no dense vegetation. Remove the lower branches of spruces, doing the pruning in late summer or fall so you don't attract spruce bark beetles. Manage this furthest zone to be natural, but try to limit how close trees and shrubs are that might spread a fire from one to the other. A trail in this zone is a good idea because it can serve as a fire break.

Sometimes access to a wooded cabin becomes difficult during a fire. Owners of vacation property in regions where wildfires are a concern often clear two access routes to the cabin to help firefighters get to it in an emergency. The driveways should be at least eighteen feet wide, made of fireproof rock or gravel and free of overhanging branches that would interfere with the approach of a fire truck. Clearly mark the entrance to your property so firefighters can find your place in an emergency. If you have a fire, you want firemen to have ready access to your home.

Other tips are pretty obvious. Stack firewood at least thirty feet from any building. Inspect your chimney and clean it regularly. Keep a spark arrestor on your chimney. Keep a clear ten-foot circle around outdoor grills. Buy fire extinguishers and check them from time to time.

This is a cursory list. For details on recommended safety and maintenance to pre-

A cabin like this with dense woods growing on all sides is at risk for fire should the weather turn dry for an extended period. It's a good idea to keep a clear zone around your vacation home to protect it.

vent losing your vacation property to fire, check with your local extension division or forestry office. Authorities in your area will be sure to have detailed instructions that will save you heartbreak or worse in case there is a fire in your area.

CHAPTER 10

SEASON'S END SHUTDOWN

MANY VACATION HOMES ARE NOISY AND ALIVE ON WEEKENDS IN SPRING, SUMMER AND FALL, AND THEN THEY ARE BUTTONED DOWN AND LEFT ALONE DURING THE WINTER MONTHS.

There are exceptions. One of the trends in the vacation homes market is toward four-season use. Some folks—cross-country ski fans, for example—might use their places more in winter than in other seasons. Still, the usual pattern is that families make many trips to their vacation properties in warmer months and then shut them down for the winter.

If you mostly use your vacation hideaway in warmer seasons, the visit you make to close down for the season is the most important single visit of the year. If you do this well, your first visit in spring will probably be pleasant and productive. You won't spend a lot of time doing damage control and you'll be able to set everything up for another summer of use without a lot of trouble.

Looking at this from the other side, failing to close down your cabin carefully can lead to heartbreak and needless expense. Sloppiness might be rewarded by animal break-ins, gas implements that refuse to start in spring, a mildewed refrigerator, burst water pipes, break-ins by human intruders, rotten food in the freezer or even a fire.

As dire as that sounds, there is no reason to get anxious about the shutdown. Once again, experience and a good checklist will get you through the process efficiently. Each home is to some degree unique; so experience will teach you what issues need to concern you during the shutdown. It is common to acquire an ever-lengthening "to-do" list for the shutdown visit. Year by year, the list gets a little longer as owners confront new messes and new problems each spring.

Why would winter be a problem? It doesn't present many threats to your primary residence, but winter threatens vacation property for two reasons.

First, there is the fact that the house will be closed up for an extended period. That means, for example, that it is more likely that critters will beat your defenses and set up housekeeping inside. If a falling tree limb breaks a window, snow and rain could blow in for many weeks before you discover the problem and deal with the mess. When you're not around using the place, things happen to a cottage.

The biggest issue is cold weather. If the house won't be heated while you are away, severe cold can affect things in ways you may not anticipate. Everyone knows that water stored will freeze if the temperatures drop low enough. If you leave a bottle or can of pop in the cabin over the winter, you may find a sticky mess when you return. In an unheated cabin in a northern or mountainous area, things freeze that you never thought could freeze. A forgotten can of beans might freeze, swell and turn to mush during a

Some water systems use pressurized air to blow water out of the pipes at the end of the vacation season. Look for a fitting like this one at the lowest point in the plumbing system.

January cold snap. Dispensers of soap can freeze. Buckets of paint might freeze. A tube of caulk can freeze and blow its container. It can get mighty cold in an unheated cabin.

Bring two lists to the cabin on your last visit. One should be a checklist of the tasks you need to complete to close the place safely. The other list will be blank at first, for it will record the things you need to accomplish and bring back next season. One list puts a cap on the season's fun and makes sure everything weathers the off-season in good condition. The other will help you bring the place back to life next season.

WATER SYSTEMS

The most important task on your last visit is to shut the water system down properly. About the worst thing that can happen over winter is for your pipes to freeze and burst. The water will then soak into various areas of the framing and freeze again, leaving you with an expensive and revolting mess. Parts of the plumbing system, such as your water heater or your water pump, could suffer damage.

It is important to know how to drain your system if you aren't sure of the best way to clean out all the water and shut your system down, hire a local repairperson or plumber to inspect your system and show you what to do. It won't be terribly expensive, and absolutely won't be as expensive as cleaning up a mess and replacing damaged plumbing and appliances.

Because different water systems have different features, no single description of the shutdown procedure will apply equally to all systems. All cottage water systems will have provisions for draining them. That is, whoever designed the water system almost surely knew about the need to drain it. Usually there is a valve on a pipe at the lowest part of the system that you turn to purge the water. You want to get all of the water out of your system, or as much as you can. Some systems use air pressure to blast out all the water.

In a typical system, you start by turning off power to the pump. Drain the water out of the water heater and the pump. Open all taps throughout the house. Open the key drain tap at the lowest part of the system. Many owners disconnect the water leads coming into and going out of the pump. If there is a filter on the line near the pump, throw it out, clean the trap and do something to remind yourself to install a new filter when you start the system up again in spring. It might take an hour or so for all the water to drain out.

If you have a pump that requires seasonal maintenance, now is the logical time to do that. The manufacturers of some pumps advise that you lubricate key spots once a year.

With the water turned off, flush all toilets. You might want to scoop or pump out as much water from the bowl as you can reach. Under every sink and faucet there will be a trap. To be completely conscientious, you should open those traps, drain them and get them back in place. If you have a dishwasher or washing machine, they might have traps that need cleaning. In general, get rid of all the water you possibly can eliminate from your system.

When you have purged your whole water system of water, dump some recreational vehicle antifreeze in each drain. Antifreeze

Before filling a drain system with antifreeze solution, it's important to remove each drain trap and empty the standing water in it.

for recreational vehicles is meant to be used in potable water systems; engine antifreeze is not. Buy nontoxic antifreeze if you have pets. The sweet-tasting antifreeze is attractive to pets, and even a small amount will kill a dog or cat. Pour a mix of about a quart of antifreeze into the each toilet through the opening that leads from the tank to the bowl. Pour about a cup of antifreeze into each drain. Push a rag into the trap of the toilet to keep sewer gases from backing into the house.

Take time to think about any liquids you plan to leave. You'll have to protect them from the cold or take them home. Some liquids, such as cleaning solutions or paints, might freeze if left in unheated spaces. A friend has built a big insulated box whose sides have four inches of hard Styrofoam. He stores all household liquids in it over the winter and has used this box for fifteen winters without suffering any accidents. He also stores spare batteries in the insulated box. Just to be safe, any liquid that you leave should be stored in a plastic bucket or ice cream container—something to contain the mess if it does freeze and explode.

APPLIANCES

Winterize all your appliances. Many people like to use this shutdown moment to clean up the exterior and interior of all appliances, replace any filters and cover the appliance.

Clean your clothes-washing machine. Close the valve on the water supply. Pour a quart of antifreeze into the washer tub. Set the washer control to "Spin" and run it for half a minute. Disconnect the electrical power. Put a little sign on the washer as a reminder that the system will have to be run with water and detergent to purge the antifreeze before it is actually used to wash clothes again. Clean and disconnect the clothes dryer. If it's a gas dryer, turn off the gas valve.

The refrigerator should be cleaned and emptied. Don't forget food that might be out of sight in a storage area in the fridge (like in the crisper, the freezer or the butter tray).

Clean the holding trays and coils on your refrigerator after shutting it off for the season.

Any food you forget is likely to greet you when you come back next spring, only it will look a whole lot worse than it did when you put it there. Unplug the refrigerator. Dump out the ice cube trays and wash them. Empty the drain pans. To avoid mildew, prop the refrigerator door open with an opened box of baking soda left as the only thing inside.

Disconnect the dishwasher and turn off the water supply. Drain the water supply lines. Disconnect the drain hose from both sides of the pump, being careful to get a bucket under it first. You might drain half a quart of water this way.

Unplug the oven and, if it's gas, turn off the gas valve. (You don't want the pilot light gas feed to be open all winter.) Clean the oven inside and out. You might want to cover it.

If you have a television set, unplug it. Appliances left plugged in are subject to being destroyed if lightning strikes the house.

OUTSIDE

Obviously, if you have a dock and ice might threaten it, you have to bring it in. Depending on the size and complexity of the dock, that can be a full day of work in itself, possibly involving several people. As mentioned earlier, it is worth studying the issue of dock construction. Even if the initial costs are higher, it makes sense to invest in a dock system that goes in and out without a whole lot of swearing and thrashing around in the water. Store the dock pieces in a safe area.

Police your grounds to see if there are any problem areas. Put away anything that could be damaged by exposure to the weather. Look for any tree limbs that threaten your cabin or the outbuildings. If a heavy limb reaches over a building, consider lopping it off.

There is nothing about cold weather that hurts two- or four-cycle gas engines, but prolonged storage and cold weather can affect the gas, and that in turn can clog gas lines and carburetors. You probably have manuals that came with your motors. The manuals will tell you what to do to winterize the devices. The main thing is to add stabilizer to the gas. With some outboard motors, you will want to remove the plugs and cycle the engine after spraying in some fogging agent.

It is obviously imperative that you leave no food behind to attract bears or pests. Throw out or take home any leftover bird food or pet food. If you want to leave bird food, store it in a tightly sealed metal container that will repel mice and squirrels.

Leave no garbage anywhere. Clean the barbecue so there is no food residue left on the grill. Bears love burned food, so even that caked-on black gunk can be attractive to them.

Consider stowing or locking up any tools. Since you won't be around for a long time, and strangers might guess that, anything you leave around (like an axe or ladder) might be too tempting to someone who figures he needs it worse than you do.

Some septic systems are subject to freezing and backing up. If the air is cold but there is no insulating blanket of snow, some septic systems freeze. This isn't usually a problem if you aren't there to use the toilet. If you might come a few times in winter you might need to consider this problem. If you place a line of bales of straw on the ground

over the drain lines, you can sometimes prevent backups due to freezing.

INSIDE MAINTENANCE

Pack up all food. Many new owners don't understand the need to do this, but with time they learn to take food home at the end of the season rather than leaving it to go bad or feed critters.

Stop to think about all the places you might have food that could go bad over the winter. Check the fridge, microwave and all storage areas. Clean out the coffee pot, throwing away the grounds. Pick up, bag or throw out any leftover pet food.

You'll feel better next spring if you do a thorough cleaning job. Follow your heart on this. I think spring is the best time to clean, as the place will get dirty over the winter whether you are there or not. It probably isn't smart to wash all your windows in fall—they'll probably need washing in spring again, anyway. Vacuum the floors and make it look nice, but the last visit of fall isn't the time to be fanatical about getting everything as clean as possible.

Clean out the woodstove or fireplace. Get rid of all the ashes so you have a clean surface to work with when you need a fire again. Close the flue and any stove pipe valve to keep bats from coming in.

If you have a problem with mice, consider putting down a series of poison dispensers. The theory of poison is that mice get thirsty when they eat it and seek water outside. Some do and some don't. But even if you return to find long-dead mice, it's better than coming back to a thriving mouse community.

Place the poison boxes along walls where you've seen evidence of mouse traffic.

By this time you should have ticked off almost all the tasks necessary to close down for the season. Meanwhile, you've been building a list of things you want to remember to bring up on the first trip in spring. Is the propane tank reasonably full or should you order more? It can be difficult to tell how much propane you have left in big tanks. On a warm day with high humidity, check the tanks early in the day. You will see a condensation line indicating the level of propane in the tanks. Do you need to buy a cord of firewood? What repair or improvement projects do you want to do next year?

Make a list and take it home with you.

Do a systematic job of securing all doors and windows. It will be a long time before you are back, and the price for leaving just one window open can be high. Lock the windows and pull the drapes. When the house will not be occupied for a long period of time, do not leave anything valuable visible to someone standing outside. It is pretty easy for a determined thief to break into most vacation homes. You aren't trying to throw up an impenetrable barrier, you are trying to leave the place so devoid of tempting items that potential thieves won't bother breaking in.

Turn off all electrical power. With some systems, you throw a lever at the power pole. On

INSPECTING & REPAIRING THE FIREBOX

Using a bright flashlight, look carefully at the bricks and mortar in the firebox **(photo A)**. If the soot is too heavy for you to see clearly, clean the firebox with a 9:1 solution of water and muriatic acid. NOTE: Always add acid to water, not water to acid. Wear protection for your hands, skin, and eyes any time you work with acid.

Remove any faulty bricks and mortar with a masonry chisel **(photo B)**. Using a stiff-bristled brush, clean the edges of the remaining bricks so that new ones will fit neatly. Apply water to the existing bricks to keep the new mortar from drying too quickly. With a bricklayer's trowel, apply mortar to the new bricks and to the surfaces where they will fit **(photo C)**. Slide the bricks in place gently until they are flush with the existing wall. Scrape off any extra mortar and let the area dry for a few minutes. Then, use a jointing tool to smooth the mortar.

Check for loose mortar in the firebox.

Chisel out loose mortar and remove faulty bricks.

"Butter" the new bricks with mortar before positioning them.

other systems, you flip all the circuit breakers.

If you have an external propane tank, screw its valve down tight.

On the way out, lock up carefully. If you stow a key on the property, make sure it is in place. Confirm that all outbuildings are securely locked and their windows are closed.

If your area gets a lot of snow, consider taking steps to deal with snow. Will your road or driveway be plowed, or is that something you need to arrange to have done? Is your roof strong enough to sustain any possible snow load, or should you have a local person occasionally knock some of the snow off?

Finally, if you have neighbors living full-time near your cabin, you might want to inform them when you have made your last visit. If you have a formal arrangement by which they swing by to check the place, you should probably see them now and make sure everyone has the same sense of how often or thoroughly they will check on things. In some vacation areas that have been highly developed, you might want to inform the police that you've closed the place down for the season.

Try to develop an attitude about the last visit. It is inherently different from the first visit. I think of the last visit as a series of tasks that must be performed, and I take satisfaction from getting through the list efficiently. But if there are optional tasks that might be better done in spring, I don't mind leaving them until then. The opening weekend trip is essentially more romantic and light-hearted. You aren't working then; you are doing a few necessary tasks in order to make it possible for your family to have a wonderful season of fun.

END OF SEASON CHECKLIST FOR COLD CLIMATES

- ❏ Shut off water and drain pipes
- ❏ Fill drain lines with antifreeze solutions
- ❏ Plug toilets with rags
- ❏ Box up all liquids for transport
- ❏ Unplug and disconnect appliances
- ❏ Clean and empty refrigerator
- ❏ Shut off gas to oven, furnace
- ❏ Remove dock, if necessary
- ❏ Store boating equipment
- ❏ Store lawn furniture
- ❏ Winterize gas lawn equipment
- ❏ Dispose of bird food, pet food
- ❏ Lock up lawn tools
- ❏ Winterize septic system
- ❏ Pack up food
- ❏ Clean cabinets, floors
- ❏ Clean ashes out of fireplace or stove
- ❏ Close fireplace flues
- ❏ Lay bait for mice
- ❏ Store bedding, linens in heavy plastic bags
- ❏ Cover furniture
- ❏ Check fuel levels on propane or oil tanks
- ❏ Secure all doors and windows
- ❏ Arrange for mail to be forwarded
- ❏ Turn off phones
- ❏ Turn off electrical power
- ❏ Close valves on propane tanks
- ❏ Make arrangements for off-season caretaking
- ❏ _____
- ❏ _____
- ❏ _____

PROJECTS

IN THIS FINAL CHAPTER YOU'LL FIND SEVEN EASY PROJECTS YOU CAN BUILD TO ACCESSORIZE YOUR VACATION HOME.

For many people, a vacation is a time to practice hobbies, and if you have a do-it-yourself personality, these projects will be recreational as well as a means to an end. All can be built with simply hand power tools, and none require advanced woodworking skills.

* *Stepping Stone Path* .... *page 124*

* *Fire Pit* .... *page 126*

* *Firewood/Garbage Shed* .... *page 130*

* *Dock Box* .... *page 138*

* *Cabin Marker* .... *page 142*

* *Cabin Porter* .... *page 146*

* *Adirondack Chair* .... *page 150*

STEPPING STONE PATH

Whether you are paving a frequently traveled area, or introducing a sense of movement to your landscape, a stepping stone path can be an ideal and inexpensive solution. A thoughtfully arranged stepping stone design almost begs to be walked upon, and its open design complements, rather than overpowers, the landscape.

When designing your path, keep in mind that paths with gentle curves or bends are usually more attractive than straight ones. The distance between the stones is also an important consideration. Set the stones to accommodate a normal stride, so you can effortlessly step from one stone to the next.

There are a variety of materials available for constructing stepping stone paths, from natural stone to prefabricated concrete. To ensure that your path blends with the rest of your landscape, select a material that suits your yard's style and existing materials. Natural stone indigenous to your area is often a good choice. Many stone yards sell 1" to 2½" sedimentary rock "steppers," which are ideal for stepping stone paths. But you can also use cut stone, wood rounds, or precast concrete pavers.

Even if you expect it to be more decorative than functional, your path should be built with methods and materials that keep safety in mind. Select stones that are wide enough to stand on comfortably and have a flat, even, lightly textured surface.

Like other paved surfaces, stepping stones can be adversely affected by the weather. Without a proper base, they can become unstable or settle unevenly. Prepare the base carefully and check the path each spring, adjusting stones as necessary for safety.

Tools & Materials

- *Spade*
- *Garden rake*
- *Stepping stones*
- *Sand or compactible gravel*

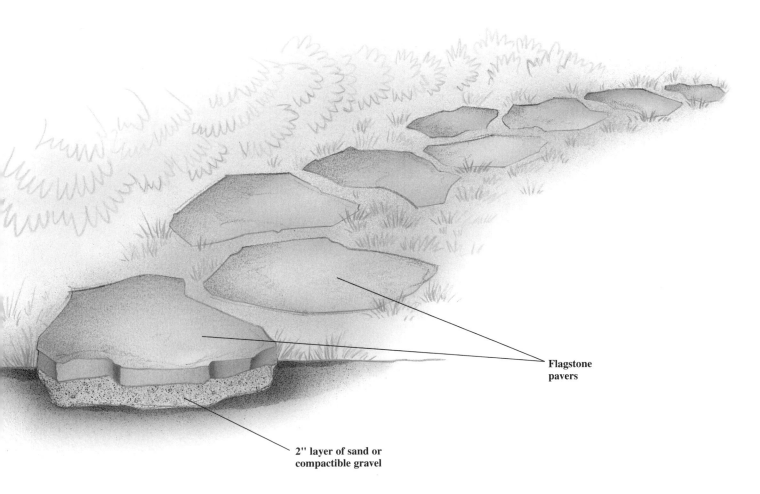

Flagstone pavers

2" layer of sand or compactible gravel

HOW TO CREATE A STEPPING STONE PATH

Step A: Arrange the Stones

Arrange the stones along the ground in your planned pattern. Walk the full course of the path, then adjust the spacing between the steppers so you can step smoothly from stone to stone.

Step B: Let the Ground Cover Die

If you're installing the path over grass or another living ground cover, leave the stones in place for three to five days. The ground cover beneath the stones will die, leaving a perfect outline of the stones.

Step C: Prepare the Base

1. Using a spade, cut around the outline, creating an excavation 2" deeper than the thickness of the stone.

2. Add a 2" layer of sand or compactible gravel and smooth it out with a garden rake.

Step D: Set & Adjust the Stones

1. Place the stones in the partially filled holes. Rock each stone back and forth several times to help it settle securely into the base.

2. Check to make sure the stones are stable and flush with the ground. Add or remove sand and readjust the stones as necessary.

Arrange the stepping stones on top of the grass, then test the layout by walking the path. Adjust the stones as necessary.

Leave the stones in place for several days to kill the grass beneath, leaving a visible outline for excavation.

Dig up the outlined areas, 2" deeper than the height of the stones. Spread a 2" layer of sand in each hole.

Reposition the stones, adding or removing sand as necessary until they're stable and flush with the ground.

FIRE PIT

A fire pit creates a unique space for enjoying fun and safe recreational fires. When determining a location for a fire pit, choose a spot where the ground is relatively flat and even, and at least 25 ft. from your home, garage, shed, or any other fixed, combustible structures in your yard. It is also important that a garden hose or other extinguishing device be accessible at the location.

In this project, two courses of 6" manhole block are used to create a fire pit with a 26" interior diameter, ideal for backyard settings within city limits. Manhole blocks are designed specifically to create rounded tunnels and walls and can be purchased from most concrete block manufacturers.

Three ¾" gaps have been factored into this design to act as air vents, allowing the natural air-flow to stoke the fire. This layout makes the circumference of the second course roughly ½" smaller than the first. A slightly thicker layer of surface-bonding cement is added to the top course to make up the difference.

Surface-bonding cement starts out as a white paste and can be tinted to match or complement any color of capstone. The 8 × 16" landscape pavers used here are cut at angles to allow ten pieces to fit around the rim of the fire pit (see illustration opposite). Pages 127 to 129 contain basic techniques for cutting and building with brick.

There are usually heavy restrictions for pit fires within city limits, regarding pit size, seasonal burning, waste burning, and more. Many municipalities also require that you purchase a recreational burning permit issued by an inspector from the fire department. Check with your local building department for restrictions specific to your area.

When not in use or during winter months, you may want to cover the top of the fire pit to prevent damage that may occur in inclement weather.

NOTE: It is important to allow your fire pit to cure for at least 30 days before building a fire in it. Heat can cause concrete with a high moisture content to greatly expand and contract, causing the material to severely crack or fragment.

- *Hammer or hand maul*
- *Tape measure*
- *Shovel*
- *Hand tamp*
- *Wheelbarrow or mixing box*
- *Mason's trowel*
- *Spray bottle*
- *Jointing tool*
- *Circular saw with an abrasive masonry blade*
- *Square-end trowel*

- *Tuck-point trowel*
- *Eye & ear protection*
- *Wire brush*
- *2 × 2 wooden stakes (2)*
- *Mason's string*
- *Spray paint*
- *Compactible gravel*
- *60-lb. concrete (12)*
- *Sheet plastic*
- *6" manhole blocks*

- *¾" wood spacers (3)*
- *Chalk*
- *Refractory mortar*
- *Surface-bonding cement*
- *Mortar tinting agent*
- *½" plywood*
- *8 × 16" landscape pavers (10)*

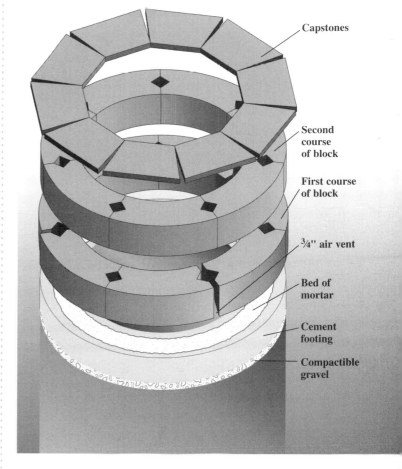

Capstones

Second course of block

First course of block

¾" air vent

Bed of mortar

Cement footing

Compactible gravel

HOW TO BUILD A FIRE PIT

Step A: Excavate the Site

1. Use a hammer or a hand maul to drive a wooden stake into the centerpoint of the planned fire pit location. Then drive a temporary stake into the ground 10½" from the center stake.

2. Tie a mason's string to the center stake—the string should be just long enough to reach the temporary stake. Hold or tie a can of spray paint to the end of the string. Pull the string taut and spray paint a circle on the ground.

3. Remove the temporary stake and drive it into the ground 22½" from the center stake. Pull the string taut, and spray a second circle on the ground.

4. Strip away the grass between the two circles and dig a trench 10" deep.

5. Fill the base of the trench with 2" of compactible gravel. Tamp the gravel thoroughly.

Step B: Pour the Footing

1. Mix concrete in a wheelbarrow or mixing box and shovel it into the trench until the concrete reaches ground level. Work the concrete with a shovel to remove any air pockets.

2. Screed the surface of the concrete by dragging a short 2 × 4 along the top of the natural form. Add concrete to any low areas and screed the surface again. Finish the concrete with a trowel.

3. When the concrete is hard to the touch, cover it with a sheet of plastic and let it cure for 2 to 3 days. Remove the plastic and let the concrete cure for an additional week.

A

Outline the location of the footing using spray paint and a piece of string. Then dig a circular trench 10" deep.

After tamping a 2" layer of compactible gravel in the bottom of the trench, fill with concrete and screed it with a scrap of 2 × 4. Float the surface with a trowel.

¾" spacer

Mist the footing with water and spread a bed of mortar inside the reference lines. Place the blocks of the first course in position, with three ¾" spacers in the course to create air vents.

¾" air vents

Dry-lay the second course of block ⅜" from the outside edge of the first course. Fill any block hollows with mortar.

Step C: Lay the First Course

1. When the concrete has sufficiently cured, lay out the first course of 6" manhole blocks with three ¾" gaps for air vents, using ¾" wood spacers.

2. Mark the internal and external circumference of the first course on the footing with chalk, and remove the blocks. Take note of any low or high spots on the footing, remembering that low spots can be leveled out with extra mortar at the base.

3. Mix a batch of refractory mortar and lightly mist the footing area with water. Throw a bed of mortar on the misted area, covering only the area inside the reference lines.

4. Set a manhole block into the bed of mortar, centering it on the footing and the chalk reference lines. Press the block into the mortar until the joint is approximately ⅜" thick. Place the second block directly against the first block with no spacing between the blocks and press it in place until the tops of the blocks are flush. Use a scrap of 2 × 4 to help you position the tops of the blocks evenly along the first course.

5. Continue laying the blocks, making sure the spaces for the three air vents are correctly positioned with the ¾" wood scraps. Do not allow the wood spacers to become set in the mortar.

6. Continue laying blocks until the first course is set. Remove any excess mortar with a trowel and finish the joints with a jointing tool.

Step D: Lay the Second Course

Dry-lay the second course of blocks over the first, offsetting the layout of the joints between the blocks. NOTE: Because of the air vents in the first course, the second course is slightly smaller in diameter. When laying the second course, line up the internal edges of the blocks, leaving a slight lip along the outer edge.

Step E: Apply Surface-bonding Cement

1. Mix a small batch of surface-bonding cement according to the manufacturer's instructions. Add a mortar tinting agent, if desired.

2. Mist the blocks of the fire pit with water. Apply the surface-bonding cement to the exterior of the fire pit walls using a square-end trowel. Make up the difference in diameter between the two courses with a thicker coating of surface-bonding cement on the second course. To even out the cement, angle the trowel slightly and make broad upward strokes. Keep the top of the fire pit clear of surface-bonding cement to ensure the cap will bond to the wall properly.

3. Use a tuck-point trowel to layer the surface-bonding cement inside the edges of the air vents. Do not cover the air vents completely with surface-bonding cement.

4. Use a wet trowel to smooth the surface to create the texture of your choice. Rinse the trowel frequently, keeping it clean and wet.

Step F: Install the Capstones

1. Make a capstone template from $\frac{1}{2}$" plywood, following the illustration (above right). Use the template to mark ten 8×16" landscape pavers to the capstone dimensions.

2. Cut the pavers to size using a circular saw with an abrasive masonry blade and a cold chisel. When cutting brick with a masonry blade, make several shallow passes, and always wear ear and eye protection.

3. Mist the top of the fire pit with water. Mix a batch of mortar and fill in any block hollows, then

throw a bed of mortar along the top of the second course.

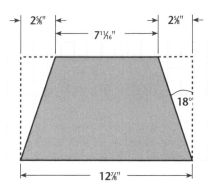

4. Butter the leading edge of each capstone, and position it on the mortar bed so the front edges overhang the interior diameter of the manhole block by roughly $\frac{1}{8}$". Adjust the capstones as you work so the joints are $\frac{3}{8}$" thick and evenly overhang the exterior edge of the pit. Also make sure the entire layer is even and level. Tool the joints as you work.

5. Use a jointing tool to smooth mortar joints within 30 minutes. Cut away any excess mortar pressed from the joints with a trowel. When the mortar is set, but not too hard, brush away excess mortar from the faces of the capstones with a wire brush.

6. Allow the fire pit to cure for 30 days before its first use.

Mist the surface of the walls and apply surface-bonding cement with a square-end trowel. Use more surface-bonding cement on the second course to even out the gap between the courses.

Lay a bed of mortar on top of the second course and set the capstones into place, maintaining a uniform overhang.

Firewood/Garbage Shed

This versatile shed is actually two projects in one: by using the same central design, you can build a firewood shelter or a garbage and recycling bin. The differences between the two are clearly shown in the illustrations below. Both projects have four posts, a rectangular floor frame decked with 2 × 6s, and spaced side slats that provide ventilation. The plywood, shed-style roof is covered with cedar shingles, but you can use any type of roofing.

When adapted as a garbage shed, the project includes a center post and slats on the rear wall, two posts on the front wall that define the door openings, a shelf for recycling, and three frame-and-panel cedar doors.

To save on expenses, you can build the entire shed with pressure-treated lumber or use cedar only for the most visible parts.

Materials

Part	Quantity/Size—Firewood Shed	Quantity/Size—Garbage Shed	Material
Framing			
Side & end floor supports	2 @ 10'-0"	2 @ 10'-0"	2 × 4 pressure-treated
Center floor support	1 @ 8'-0"	1 @ 8'-0"	2 × 4 pressure-treated
Floor boards	3 @ 10'-0"	3 @ 10'-0"	2 × 6 pressure-treated
Corner posts	4 @ 8'-0"	4 @ 8'-0"	2 × 4 cedar
Headers	2 @ 8'-0"	2 @ 8'-0"	2 × 4 cedar
Rafters	1 @ 8'-0", 1 @ 4'-0"	1 @ 8'-0", 1 @ 4'-0"	2 × 4 cedar
Rear center post		1 @ 4'-0"	2 × 4 cedar
Door posts		1 @ 8'-0"	2 × 4 cedar
Door ledger		1 @ 8'-0"	2 × 4 cedar
Slats			
End slats	5 @ 8'-0"	5 @ 8'-0"	1 × 6 cedar
Back slats		5 @ 8'-0"	1 × 6 cedar
Roofing			
Sheathing	1 sheet @ 4 × 8'	1 sheet @ 4 × 8'	¾" CDX plywood
Roof edging	2 @ 10'-0"	2 @ 10'-0"	1 × 2 cedar
15# building paper	37 sq. ft.	37 sq. ft.	
Shingles	25 sq. ft	25 sq. ft.	18" cedar shingles
Roof cap	1 @ 8'-0"	1 @ 8'-0"	1 × 4 cedar
	1 @ 8'-0"	1 @ 8'-0"	1 × 3 cedar
Shelf & Doors			
Shelf		1 @ 24⅝ × 28⅛"	¾" ext.-grade plywood
Shelf cleats		1 @ 6'-0"	1 × 3 cedar
Door panels		1 sheet @ 4 × 8'	½" rough cedar plywood
Stiles		3 @ 8'-0" (wide doors) 1 @ 10'-0" (narrow door)	1 × 4 cedar
Hinges		6	Exterior hinges
Door handles		3	Exterior handles
Fasteners			
¼" × 3" lag screws	8, with washers	10, with washers	
Deck screws:			
3½"	12	12	
3"	62	62	
2½"	36	48	
2"	50	62	
1⅝"	100	160	
1¼"		16	
1"		100	
6d galvanized finish nails	30	30	
3d galvanized roofing nails	1 lb.	1 lb.	

FLOOR FRAMING PLAN

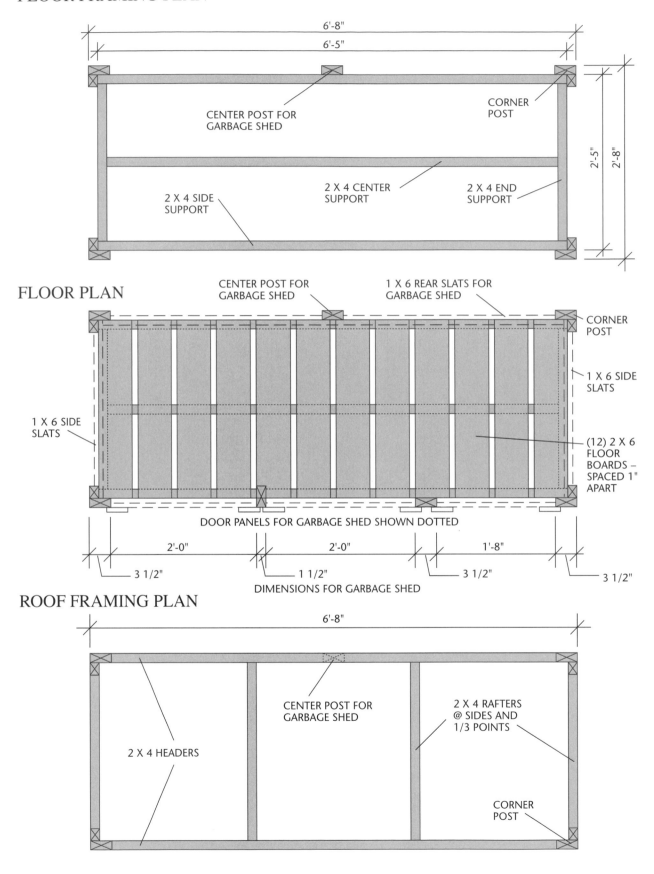

6'-8"

6'-5"

CENTER POST FOR
GARBAGE SHED

CORNER
POST

2 X 4 SIDE
SUPPORT

2 X 4 CENTER
SUPPORT

2 X 4 END
SUPPORT

2'-5"

2'-8"

FLOOR PLAN

CENTER POST FOR
GARBAGE SHED

1 X 6 REAR SLATS FOR
GARBAGE SHED

CORNER
POST

1 X 6 SIDE
SLATS

1 X 6 SIDE
SLATS

(12) 2 X 6
FLOOR
BOARDS –
SPACED 1"
APART

DOOR PANELS FOR GARBAGE SHED SHOWN DOTTED

2'-0"

2'-0"

1'-8"

3 1/2"

1 1/2"

3 1/2"

3 1/2"

DIMENSIONS FOR GARBAGE SHED

ROOF FRAMING PLAN

6'-8"

CENTER POST FOR
GARBAGE SHED

2 X 4 RAFTERS
@ SIDES AND
1/3 POINTS

2 X 4 HEADERS

CORNER
POST

BUILDING SECTION

RAFTER TEMPLATES

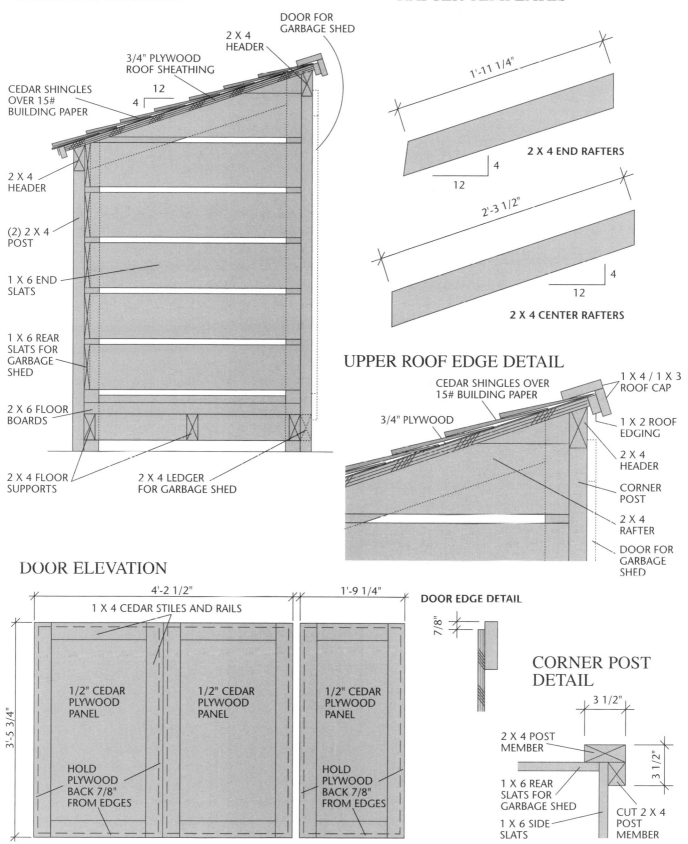

DOOR FOR GARBAGE SHED

2 X 4 HEADER

3/4" PLYWOOD ROOF SHEATHING

CEDAR SHINGLES OVER 15# BUILDING PAPER

12

4

2 X 4 HEADER

(2) 2 X 4 POST

1 X 6 END SLATS

1 X 6 REAR SLATS FOR GARBAGE SHED

2 X 6 FLOOR BOARDS

2 X 4 FLOOR SUPPORTS

2 X 4 LEDGER FOR GARBAGE SHED

1'-11 1/4"

2 X 4 END RAFTERS

4

12

2'-3 1/2"

4

12

2 X 4 CENTER RAFTERS

UPPER ROOF EDGE DETAIL

CEDAR SHINGLES OVER 15# BUILDING PAPER

3/4" PLYWOOD

1 X 4 / 1 X 3 ROOF CAP

1 X 2 ROOF EDGING

2 X 4 HEADER

CORNER POST

2 X 4 RAFTER

DOOR FOR GARBAGE SHED

DOOR ELEVATION

4'-2 1/2"

1'-9 1/4"

1 X 4 CEDAR STILES AND RAILS

3'-5 3/4"

1/2" CEDAR PLYWOOD PANEL

1/2" CEDAR PLYWOOD PANEL

1/2" CEDAR PLYWOOD PANEL

HOLD PLYWOOD BACK 7/8" FROM EDGES

HOLD PLYWOOD BACK 7/8" FROM EDGES

DOOR EDGE DETAIL

7/8"

CORNER POST DETAIL

3 1/2"

2 X 4 POST MEMBER

3 1/2"

1 X 6 REAR SLATS FOR GARBAGE SHED

1 X 6 SIDE SLATS

CUT 2 X 4 POST MEMBER

FRONT ELEVATION

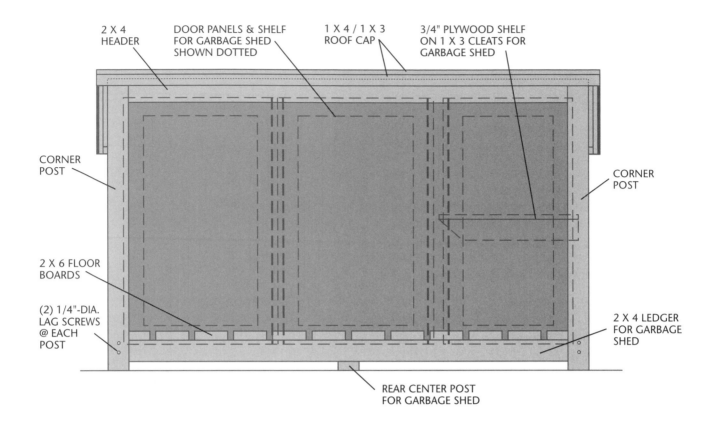

2 X 4
HEADER

DOOR PANELS & SHELF
FOR GARBAGE SHED
SHOWN DOTTED

1 X 4 / 1 X 3
ROOF CAP

3/4" PLYWOOD SHELF
ON 1 X 3 CLEATS FOR
GARBAGE SHED

CORNER
POST

CORNER
POST

2 X 6 FLOOR
BOARDS

2 X 4 LEDGER
FOR GARBAGE
SHED

(2) 1/4"-DIA.
LAG SCREWS
@ EACH
POST

REAR CENTER POST
FOR GARBAGE SHED

REAR ELEVATION

SIDE ELEVATION

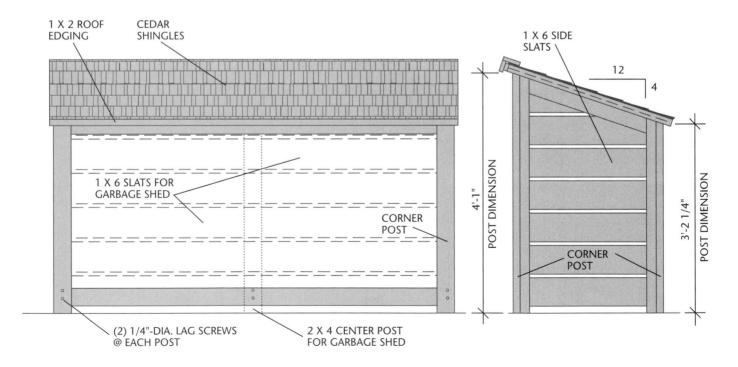

1 X 2 ROOF
EDGING

CEDAR
SHINGLES

1 X 6 SIDE
SLATS

12

4

1 X 6 SLATS FOR
GARBAGE SHED

CORNER
POST

4'-1"
POST DIMENSION

3'-2 1/4"
POST DIMENSION

CORNER
POST

(2) 1/4"-DIA. LAG SCREWS
@ EACH POST

2 X 4 CENTER POST
FOR GARBAGE SHED

BUILDING THE FIREWOOD/GARBAGE SHED

Step A: Build the Floor Frame

1. Cut the two side supports at 77" and the two end supports at 26". Cut the center support at 74".

2. Fasten the ends between the sides with 3½" deck screws driven through the sides into the ends, following the FLOOR FRAMING PLAN on page 132. Position the screws where they won't interfere with the lag screws that will anchor the corner posts to the floor frame (see the FRONT and REAR ELEVATIONS, on page 134). Fasten the center support between the ends so it's centered between the side supports.

3. Cut twelve 2 × 6 floor boards at 29". Make sure the floor frame is square by measuring diagonally from corner to corner: The frame is square when the measurements are equal. Starting at one end, place the first board flush with the side and end supports. Drill pilot holes and attach the board with 3" deck screws.

4. Cut two 1" spacers from scrap lumber and use them to install the remaining floor boards. If you are building the garbage shed, cut a 1½"-wide × 2"-deep notch for the left door post, starting 26" from the left end of the floor frame. If necessary, rip the final board so it's flush with the end support.

Step B: Build & Install the Corner Posts

NOTE: Each corner post is made from one full-width 2 × 4 and one 2 × 4 ripped to 2"; the boards are screwed together to form an L. The top ends of both boards are cut at an 18° angle to match the roof slope. The garbage shed also has a center post—made from a single 2 × 4—at the rear side of the frame (this is installed in Step C).

1. Rip two 8-ft.-long 2 × 4s to 2" in width. Make an 18° angled cut at about 53", leaving one 43" piece from each. Cut two full-width 2 × 4s at 53" and two at 43", beveling the top ends at 18°.

2. Assemble each front post by placing the cut edge of one 53"-long ripped board against the face of a 53" 2 × 4 so their angled ends are flush (see the FLOOR PLAN, on page 132 and the CORNER POST DETAIL, on page 133). Drill pilot holes and join the pieces with 3" deck screws driven through the full-width 2 × 4 and into the ripped piece. Assemble the two rear posts the same way.

3. Cut the posts to length with square cuts: Cut the front posts at 49", measuring from the longest point of the angled ends; cut the rear posts at 38¼", measuring from the shortest point of the angled ends.

4. Mark the insides of the posts 1½" from the ends. Position each post on the floor frame so the mark is aligned with the bottom edge of the frame. Use a framing square to make sure the post is perpendicular to the frame and clamp the post in place. Drill counterbored pilot holes for the lag screws and washers and fasten each post with two ¼" × 3" lag screws.

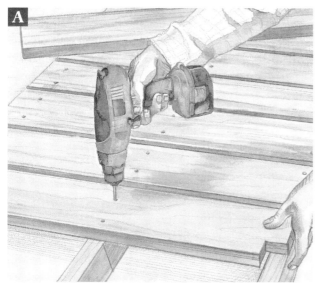

Attach the floor boards to the frame, setting 1" gaps. For the garbage shed, cut a notch for the left door post.

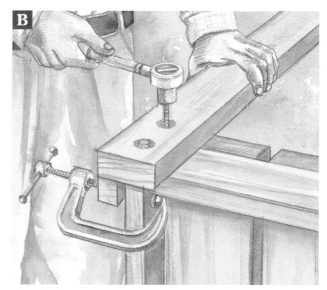

Attach the posts to the floor frame with lag screws driven through pilot holes counterbored to accept the lag washers.

Step C: Frame the Roof

1. Cut two 2 × 4 roof headers at 73". Bevel the top edge of each header at 18° (the broader face should still measure $3\frac{1}{2}$" after the board is beveled).

2. Position the headers between the corner posts so their outside faces are flush with the outside post faces and their beveled edges are flush with the tops of the posts. Toescrew the headers to the posts with $2\frac{1}{2}$" deck screws.

3. Cut two of each type of 2 × 4 rafters, following the RAFTER TEMPLATES, on page 133. Position the outer rafters between the corner posts so their outside faces and top edges are flush with the out-sides and tops of the posts. Toescrew the rafters to the posts with $2\frac{1}{2}$" deck screws.

4. Position the two inner rafters between the headers, 25" in from the outer rafters. Toescrew the rafters in place with $2\frac{1}{2}$" deck screws.

5. If you're building the garbage shed, cut the 2 × 4 rear center post to length so it runs from the bottom edge of the rear header to $1\frac{1}{2}$" below the bottom of the floor frame. Install the center post, centered between the corner posts; anchor the bottom end to the floor frame with lag screws, and toescrew the top end to the rear header.

Step D: Add the 1 × 6 Slats

NOTE: The firewood shed has slats along the ends only; the garbage shed has slats along the ends and back side. Determining the size of the gap between slats is up to you—test your layout carefully before installing the slats.

1. On each end, cut the bottom slat to fit between the corner posts. Position the slat between the posts so its bottom edge is flush with the bottom of the floor frame and fasten it to the frame with $1\frac{5}{8}$" deck screws.

2. Cut the remaining slats to fit between the insides of the posts. Space the slats as desired, and fasten them to the posts with $1\frac{5}{8}$" deck screws driven through the backs of the slats and into the posts.

3. If you're building the garbage shed, install two bottom slats between the center post and the two corner posts, keeping their bottom edges flush with the floor frame. Install the remaining slats against the insides of the posts.

Step E: Install the Sheathing & Roofing

1. Cut the $\frac{3}{4}$" plywood roof sheathing at $35\frac{1}{2}$ × $81\frac{1}{2}$". Position the sheathing over the roof frame so it overhangs the posts by $\frac{3}{4}$" on all sides. Secure the sheathing to the posts, headers, and rafters with 2" deck screws.

2. Add 1 × 2 trim along all edges of the sheathing, mitering the ends at the corners. Fasten the trim with 6d galv. finish nails so the top edges are flush with the plywood.

3. Apply 15# building paper to the sheathing and

Fasten the outer rafters between the posts with screws. Drive two screws on the inside face and one at the bottom.

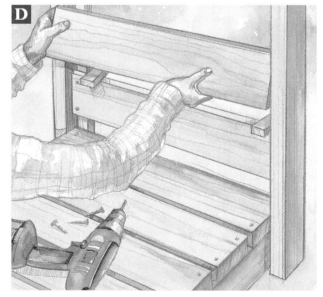

Attach the end slats to the inside faces of the corner posts. Set consistent gaps between all of the slats.

edging. Overhang the bottom edge by 1" and the sides by ½". Install the cedar shingles.

4. Build the roof cap from a cedar 1 × 3 and 1 × 4. Cut both pieces to span the length of the roof along the front edge. Set the 1 × 4 over the edge of the 1 × 3 and nail them together with 6d galvanized finish nails.

NOTE: If you're building the firewood shed, you have finished. If you're building the garbage shed, you have two more steps to go.

Step F: Complete the Garbage Shed Framing

1. Cut the 2 × 4 door ledger at 73". Position the ledger between the front corner posts so its top edge is flush with the top edge of the side support of the floor frame. Fasten the ledger with 2½" deck screws driven through the side support and into the ledger.

2. Cut the 2 × 4 door posts to fit between the ledger and the front header. Position the door posts following the FLOOR FRAMING PLAN on page 132 (note that the left post is on-edge and the right post is flat). Make sure the posts are plumb, and fasten them with 2½" deck screws.

Step G: Add the Shelf & Doors

1. Mark the positions of the shelf cleats onto the inside faces of the rear, side and end slats and the right door post. Measure up from the shed floor and make marks at 17".

2. Cut the 1 × 3 shelf cleats, one each at 26½",

24½", and 3½". Position the cleats with their top edges on the 17" height marks, and fasten them to the slats and post with 1¼" deck screws.

3. Cut the ¾" plywood shelf at 24⅝ × 28⅛". Fasten the shelf to the cleats with 1⅝" deck screws.

4. Cut the 1 × 4 pieces for the door frames: From three 8-ft. 1 × 4s, cut four stiles at 41¾" and four rails at 18¼"; from one 10-ft. 1 × 4, cut two stiles at 41¾" and two rails at 14¼". Cut the door panels from ½" cedar plywood: two panels at 23½ × 40" and one panel at 19½ × 40".

5. Assemble the doors following the DOOR ELEVATION, on page 133. To assemble each door, place the frame pieces facedown, with the rails between the stiles. Set the door panel facedown over the frame so there is ⅞" between the edge of the panel and the frame on all sides. Fasten the pieces together with 1" deck screws driven through the panel and into the frame pieces. Use a framing square to make sure the frame is square as you work.

6. Attach hinges and handles to the doors. Install the doors on the shed so they overlap the openings by ⅝" on all sides. NOTE: Use exterior hinges. A sash hinge with an offset that matches the thickness of the door stiles works well. To use standard strap hinges, mount the hinges on blocks attached to the door posts, so the doors can open all the way.

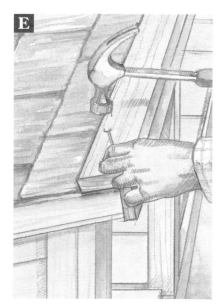

Cover the shingle ends at the top edge of the roof with a 1 × roof cap.

Install the door posts flush with the door ledger and header.

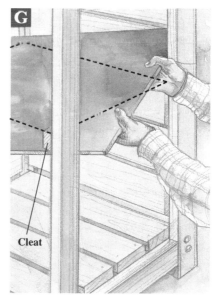

Add cleats to the door post and side and rear walls, then install the shelf.

DOCK BOX

With its spacious storage compartment and appealing nautical design, this box is a perfect place for stowing water sports equipment. You won't have to haul gear inside anymore after off-shore excursions. Life preservers, beach toys, ropes and even small coolers conveniently fit inside this attractive chest, which has ventilation holes to discourage mildew. Sturdy enough for seating, the large top can hold charts, fishing gear or a light snack while you await your next voyage. With a dock box to hold your gear, you can spend your energy carrying more important items—like the fresh catch of the day—up to your cabin.

Construction Materials	
Quantity	**Lumber**
2	⅝" × 4 × 8' plywood siding
7	1 × 2" × 8' cedar
4	1 × 4" × 8' cedar
1	1 × 6" × 8' cedar
3	2 × 2" × 8' cedar

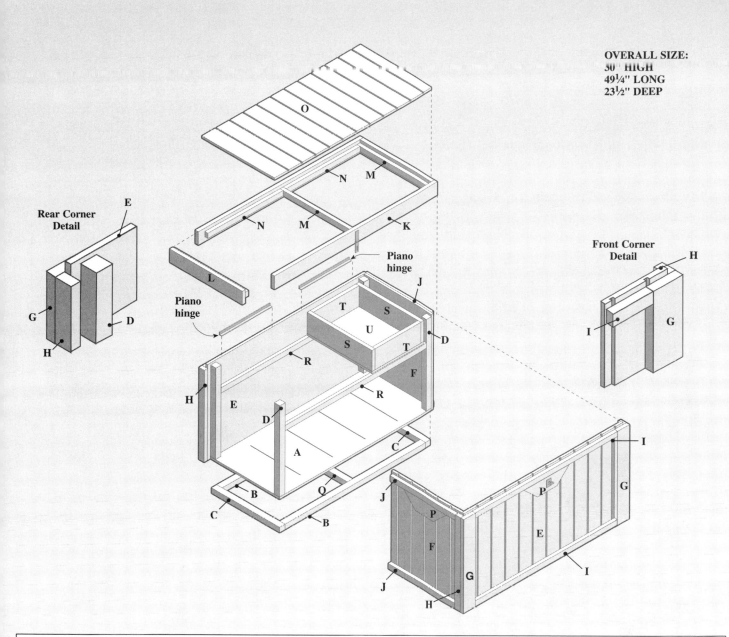

Rear Corner Detail

Front Corner Detail

Piano hinge

Piano hinge

Key	Part	Dimension	Pcs.	Material
A	Bottom	⅝ × 46¼ × 20½"	1	Plywood siding
B	Bottom brace	1½ × 1½ × 43¼"	2	Cedar
C	End brace	1½ × 1½ × 20½"	2	Cedar
D	Corner brace	1½ × 1½ × 24⅜"	4	Cedar
E	Large panel	⅝ × 47½ × 27"	2	Plywood siding
F	Small panel	⅝ × 20½ × 27"	2	Plywood siding
G	Corner trim	⅞ × 3½ × 26½"	4	Cedar
H	Corner batten	⅞ × 1½ × 26½"	4	Cedar
I	Long trim	⅞ × 1½ × 42¼"	4	Cedar
J	End trim	⅞ × 1½ × 18¾"	4	Cedar
K	Lid side	⅞ × 3½ × 49¼"	2	Cedar

Key	Part	Dimension	Pcs.	Material
L	Lid end	⅞ × 3½ × 21¾"	2	Cedar
M	Top support	⅞ × 1½ × 21¾"	3	Cedar
N	Ledger	⅞ × 1½ × 22⅜"	4	Cedar
O	Top panel	⅝ × 47½ × 21¾"	1	Plywood siding
P	Handle	⅞ × 3½ × 13½"	4	Cedar
Q	Cross brace	1½ × 1½ × 17½	1	Cedar
R	Tray slide	⅞ × 1½ × 43¼"	2	Cedar
S	Tray side	⅞ × 5½ × 20¼"	2	Cedar
T	Tray end	⅞ × 5½ × 14"	2	Cedar
U	Tray bottom	⅝ × 15¾ × 20¼"	1	Plywood siding

Materials: 1¼" and 1⅝" deck screws, 6d finish nails, 1" wire brads, construction adhesive, 1½ × 30" or 36" piano hinge, hasp, lid support chains (2), finishing materials.

Note: Measurements reflect the actual size of dimension lumber.

HOW TO BUILD A DOCK BOX

Make the box bottom.

The box bottom is made of grooved plywood siding attached to a rectangular 2 × 2 box frame.

1. Cut the bottom (A), bottom braces (B), end braces (C) and cross brace (Q) to size. Apply construction adhesive or moisture-resistant wood glue to the ends of the bottom braces. Clamp them between the end braces so the edges are flush. Drill $\frac{1}{8}$" pilot holes through each end brace into the bottom braces. Counterbore the holes $\frac{1}{4}$" deep, using a counterbore bit. Drive $1\frac{5}{8}$" deck screws through the pilot holes to reinforce the joints.

2. Center the cross brace in the frame and attach it with adhesive and $1\frac{5}{8}$" deck screws.

3. Attach the box bottom to the box frame with $1\frac{5}{8}$" deck screws.

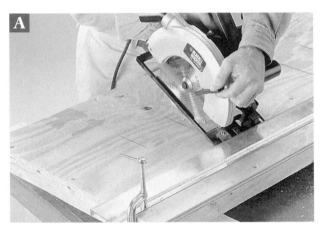

For ventilation, cut slots into the bottom panel, using a straightedge as a stop block for the foot of your circular saw.

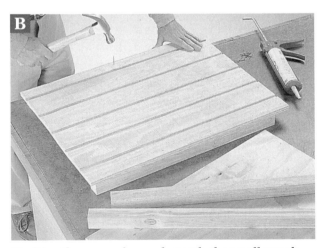

Position the corner braces beneath the small panels, and fasten them with adhesive and finish nails.

4. Cut six ventilation slots in the bottom panel. First, clamp a straightedge near one edge of the bottom panel. Then, set the cutting depth on your circular saw to about 1" and press the foot of the saw up against the straightedge. Turn on the saw, and press down with the blade in a rocking motion until you've cut through the bottom panel (**photo A**). The slots should be spaced evenly, 8" to 9" apart.

Attach the box sides.

1. Cut the corner braces (D), large panels (E) and small panels (F) to size. Align two corner braces under a small panel (grooved side up). Make sure the edges are flush, with a $\frac{1}{2}$"-wide gap at one end of the panel and a $2\frac{1}{8}$"-wide gap at the other end. Fasten the braces with construction adhesive and 6d finish nails (**photo B**).

2. Repeat the procedure for the other small panel.

3. Attach the small panels, with the 2" space facing downward, to the end braces, using 6d nails and construction adhesive.

4. Place the large panels in position and drive nails through the panels into the bottom braces and corner braces.

Make the trim pieces.

1. Cut the corner trim (G) and corner battens (H) to length. Set the project on its side. Use construction adhesive and nails to attach the corner battens flush with the bottom, covering the seam between panels. There should be a $\frac{1}{2}$"-wide gap between the tops of the corner pieces and the top of the box. Then, attach the corner trim (**photo C**).

2. Cut the long trim (I) and the end trim (J) to

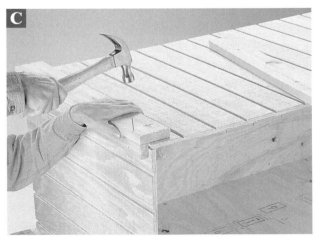

Attach the corner trim pieces flush with the edges of the corner battens to cover the plywood joints.

length. Attach the lower trim flush with the bottom, using construction adhesive and finish nails.

3. Attach the upper trim pieces flush with the corner pieces, using adhesive. Drive 1¼" deck screws from inside the box into the trim pieces.

Attach the handles.
The handles (P) are trapezoid-shaped blocks cut from cedar.

1. Cut four handles to length. Mark each piece 3¾" in from each end along one long edge. Connect the marks diagonally to the adjacent corners to form cutting lines. Cut with a circular saw or a power miter box.

2. Center a handle against the bottom edge of the top trim piece on each face. Attach each handle with adhesive and 1¼" deck screws **(photo D)**.

Make the tray.
The tray rests inside the dock box on slides.

1. Cut the tray slides (R) to length. Mount the slides inside the box, 7" down from the top edge, using adhesive and 1¼" deck screws.

2. Cut the tray sides (S), tray ends (T) and tray bottom (U) to size. Drill pilot holes in the tray ends and counterbore the holes. Then, fasten the tray ends between the tray sides with adhesive and 1⅝" deck screws **(photo E)**. Attach the tray bottom with adhesive and 1" wire brads.

Make the lid.
1. Cut the lid sides (K) and lid ends (L) to length. Fasten them together with adhesive and drive 6d nails through the lid sides and into the ends.

2. Cut the top panel (O), top supports (M) and ledgers (N) to length. Attach two top supports to the inside edges of the frame, ⅝" down from the top edge, using adhesive and 1¼" screws **(photo F)**. Attach the ledgers to the long sides of the lid—one at each corner—with adhesive and 1¼" deck screws. Place the remaining top support into the gap in the middle. Fasten it by driving 6d nails into the ends of the support.

3. Fit the top panel into the lid. Fasten with 6d nails and adhesive. Sand all exposed edges.

4. Attach the lid to the box with a piano hinge cut in two. Attach a pair of chains between the bottom of the lid and the front of the box to hold the lid upright when open. To lock the box, attach a hasp to the handle and lid at the front of the box.

5. Apply exterior stain or water sealer for protection. Caulk the gap around the top panel and lid frame with exterior caulk.

A handle block is attached to each face of the box, up against the bottom of the top trim piece.

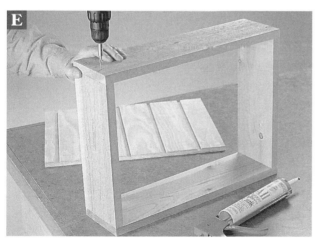

Counterbore the screw heads so they don't obstruct the movement of the tray on the tray slides.

Top supports in the lid frame support the top panel.

CABIN MARKER

Trips to a friend's cabin or vacation home, though usually enjoyable, often start on a confusing note. "Do you have the address written down?" is a common refrain after the fourth left into a dead end in the woods. You can save your friends confusion and wasted time by displaying your name, address and mailbox at the head of your driveway. And on a safety note, emergency vehicles can spot your home more quickly with a well-marked name and address on it. The simple design of this cabin marker and mailbox stand makes it suitable for almost any yard. Its height ensures a certain level of prominence, but the cedar material and basic construction allow it to fit right in with its natural surroundings. One of the best features of the cabin marker may be the least noticed—the base section. The base is a multi-tiered pyramid of 4 × 4 cedar timbers. It provides ample weight and stability, so you won't need to go to the trouble of digging a hole or pouring concrete. Just position the marker wherever you want it, and stake it in place. Much more attractive than a simple mailbox stand, this project will provide just the touch of originality that your cabin or vacation home deserves.

Construction Materials	
Quantity	**Lumber**
1	1 × 6" × 8' cedar
1	2 × 2" × 6' cedar
4	2 × 4" × 8' cedar
3	4 × 4" × 8' cedar

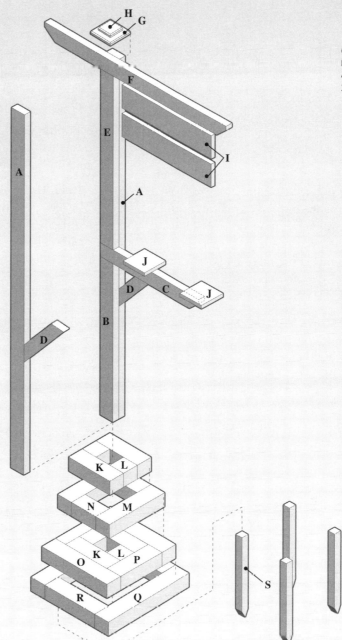

Cutting List

Key	Part	Dimension	Pcs.	Material
A	Post side	1½ × 3½ × 84"	2	Cedar
B	Post section	1½ × 3½ × 36½"	1	Cedar
C	Mailbox arm	1½ × 3½ × 23½"	1	Cedar
D	Mailbox brace	1½ × 3½ × 17½"	2	Cedar
E	Post section	1½ × 3½ × 40½"	1	Cedar
F	Sign arm	1½ × 3½ × 48½"	1	Cedar
G	Top plate	⅞ × 5½ × 5½"	1	Cedar
H	Cap	⅞ × 3½ × 3½"	1	Cedar
I	Sign board	⅞ × 5½ × 24"	2	Cedar
J	Mailbox cleat	⅞ × 5½ × 5⅞"	2	Cedar

Cutting List

Key	Part	Dimension	Pcs.	Material
K	Base piece	3½ × 3½ × 10½"	4	Cedar
L	Base piece	3½ × 3½ × 4½"	4	Cedar
M	Base piece	3½ × 3½ × 15"	2	Cedar
N	Base piece	3½ × 3½ × 7"	2	Cedar
O	Base piece	3½ × 3½ × 17½"	2	Cedar
P	Base piece	3½ × 3½ × 11½"	2	Cedar
Q	Base piece	3½ × 3½ × 22"	2	Cedar
R	Base piece	3½ × 3½ × 14"	2	Cedar
S	Stake	1½ × 1½ × 18"	4	Cedar

Materials: Moisture-resistant glue, epoxy glue, 2", 2½" and 4" deck screws, #10 screw eyes (8), S-hooks (4), ⅜"-dia. × 5" galvanized lag screws with 1" washers (8), finishing materials.
Note: Measurements reflect the actual size of dimension lumber.

HOW TO BUILD A CABIN MARKER

Make the post.

The post is made in three layers. Two post sections and two arms form the central layer, which is sandwiched between two post sides. The arms extend out from the post to support a mailbox and an address sign.

1. Cut the mailbox arm (C) and sign arm (F) to length. One end of the mailbox arm and both ends of the sign arm are cut with decorative slants on their bottom edges. To cut the ends of the arms to shape, mark a point on the three ends, 1" down from a long edge. On the opposite long edge, mark a point on the face $2\frac{1}{2}$" in from the end. Draw a straight line connecting the points, and cut along it.

2. Cut the post sides (A) and post sections (B, E) to length. To assemble the post, you will sandwich the sections and the arms between the sides. Set one of the post sides on a flat work surface, and position the lower post section (B) on top of it, face to face, with the ends flush. Attach the lower post section to the side with wood glue and $2\frac{1}{2}$" deck screws.

3. Position the mailbox arm on the side, making sure the square end is flush with the edge of the side. Use a square to make sure the mailbox arm is perpendicular to the side. Attach the mailbox arm, using glue and $2\frac{1}{2}$" deck screws.

4. Butt the end of the upper post section (E) against the top edge of the mailbox arm, and attach it to the side in the same manner (**photo A**).

5. Position the sign arm at the top of the assembly so it extends 30" past the post on the side with the mailbox arm. Attach the sign arm to the post side with glue and deck screws.

6. Apply glue to the remaining side. Attach it to the post sections with glue and 4" deck screws, making sure all the ends are flush.

Attach the mailbox cleats and braces.

The cleats on the mailbox arm provide a stable nailing surface for a "rural-style" mailbox. The mailbox braces fasten to the post and mailbox arm to provide support.

1. Cut the mailbox cleats (J) to length and sand smooth. Center the cleats on the top of the mailbox arm. The frontmost cleat should overhang the front of the mailbox arm by 1". Center the remaining cleat $12\frac{1}{2}$" in from the front of the mailbox arm. Attach the cleats with glue and $2\frac{1}{2}$" deck screws.

2. Cut the mailbox braces (D) to length. Their ends must be cut at an angle. Use a power miter box, or a backsaw and miter box, to miter-cut each end of each mailbox brace at a 45° angle. Make sure the cuts at either end slant toward each other (see Diagram, page 143).

3. Position a mailbox brace against the side of the mailbox arm so one end is flush with the top edge of the mailbox arm and the other rests squarely against the post. Drill $\frac{1}{8}$" pilot holes. Counterbore the holes $\frac{1}{4}$" deep, using a counterbore bit. Attach the mailbox braces with glue and $2\frac{1}{2}$" deck screws (**photo B**).

Butt an end of the upper section against the top edge of the mailbox arm, and fasten it to the side.

Position a mailbox brace on each side of the mailbox arm, and fasten them to the post and arm.

Complete the post top.

The post assembly is capped with a post top and cap made of 1" dimension lumber.

1. Cut the top plate (G) and cap (H) to size. Using a power sander, make ¼"-wide × ¼"-deep bevels along the top edges of the top and cap.

2. Center the top on the post, and attach it with glue and 2" deck screws. Center the cap on the top and attach it **(photo C)**.

Make the base.

The base for the cabin marker is made from cedar frames that increase in size from top to bottom. The frames are stacked to create a four-level pyramid. A fifth frame fits inside one of the frames to make a stabilizer for the post. The bottom frame is fastened to stakes driven into the ground to provide a secure anchor that does not require digging holes and pouring concrete footings.

1. Cut the 4 × 4 base pieces (K, L, M, N, O, P, Q, R) to length for all five frames. Assemble them into five frames according to the Diagram, page 143. To join the pieces, use 4" deck screws driven into pilot holes that have been counterbored 1½" deep.

2. After all five frames are built, join one of the small frames and the two next-smallest frames together in a pyramid, using glue and 4" deck screws **(photo D)**. Insert the other small frame into the opening in the third-smallest frame. Secure with deck screws.

3. Set the base assembly on top of the large frame; do not attach them. Insert the post into the opening, and secure it with lag screws, driven through the top frame and into the post. (NOTE: The bottom frame is anchored to the ground on site before being attached to the pyramid.)

Make the sign boards.

1. Cut the sign boards (I) to size. Sand them smooth.

2. Stencil your name and address onto the signs. Or, you can use adhesive letters, freehand painting, a router with a veining bit or a woodburner. Be sure to test the technique on a sanded scrap of cedar before working on the signs.

Apply finishing touches.

1. Join the two signs together with #10 screw eyes and S-hooks. Drill pilot holes for the screw eyes in the sign arm and signs. Apply epoxy glue to the threads of the screws before inserting them. Apply your finish of choice.

2. Position the bottom frame of the base in the desired location. The area should be flat and level so the post is plumb. Check the frame with a level. Add or remove dirt around the base to achieve a level base before installing.

3. Cut the stakes (S) to length, and sharpen one end of each stake. Set the stakes in the inside corners of the frame. Drive them into the ground until the tops are lower than the tops of the frame. Attach the stakes to the frames with 4" deck screws.

4. Center the cabin marker on the bottom frame. Complete the base by driving 5" lag screws through the tops of the base into the bottom frame.

Apply glue to the bottom face of the cap, and center it on the top of the post.

Attach the base tiers to each other, working from top to bottom.

CABIN PORTER

Transporting luggage and supplies doesn't need to be an awkward, backbreaking exercise. Simply roll this cabin porter to your car when you arrive, load it up and wheel your gear to your cabin door or down to the dock. The porter is spacious enough to hold coolers, laundry baskets or grocery bags, all in one easy, convenient trip. Both end gates are removable, so you can transport longer items like skis, ladders or lumber for improvement projects. The cabin porter is also handy for moving heavy objects around your yard. The 10" wheels ensure a stable ride, and the porter is designed to minimize the chances of tipping. The wheels, axle and mounting hardware generally can be purchased as a set from a well-stocked hardware store. For winter use, you might try adding short skis or sled runners, allowing the cabin porter to glide over deep snow and decreasing your chances of dropping an armful of supplies over slippery ice.

Construction Materials	
Quantity	Lumber
3	2 × 4" × 8' cedar
11	1 × 4" × 8' cedar

OVERALL SIZE:
24½" HIGH
28½" WIDE
73¾" LONG

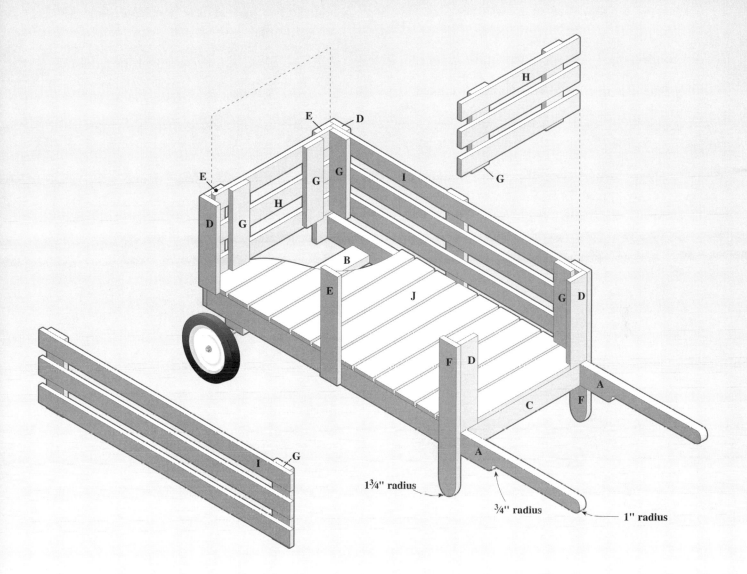

1¾" radius

¾" radius

1" radius

Cutting List				
Key	**Part**	**Dimension**	**Pcs.**	**Material**
A	Handle	1½ × 3½ × 72⅞"	2	Cedar
B	Front stringer	1½ × 3½ × 24"	1	Cedar
C	Rear stringer	1½ × 3½ × 21"	1	Cedar
D	Short stile	⅞ × 3½ × 14⅜"	4	Cedar
E	Long stile	⅞ × 3½ × 17⅞"	4	Cedar

Cutting List				
Key	**Part**	**Dimension**	**Pcs.**	**Material**
F	Rear stile	⅞ × 3½ × 24½"	2	Cedar
G	Gate stile	⅞ × 3½ × 13½"	8	Cedar
H	Gate rail	⅞ × 3½ × 22"	6	Cedar
I	Side rail	⅞ × 3½ × 46⅝"	6	Cedar
J	Slat	⅞ × 3½ × 24"	12	Cedar

Materials: 1½", 2", and 2½" deck screws, wood glue, 10"-dia. wheels (2), axle, ¾ × 4" metal straps (3), ¼ × 1" lag screws, washers, crimp caps, finishing materials.
Note: Measurements reflect the actual size of dimension lumber.

HOW TO BUILD A CABIN PORTER

Assemble the handles and framework.
The framework for the cabin porter consists of handles connected by stringers at each end.

1. Cut the handles (A), front stringer (B) and rear stringer (C) to length. Sand the edges smooth.

2. Trim the back ends of the handles to create gripping surfaces. Draw a 16"-long cutting line on the face of each handle, starting at one end, $1\frac{1}{2}$" up from the bottom edge. Set the point of a compass at the bottom edge, $14\frac{1}{2}$" in from the end, and draw a $1\frac{1}{2}$"-radius arc, creating a smooth curve leading up to the cut line. To round the ends of each handle, use a compass to draw a 1"-radius semicircle centered 1" below the top edge and 1" in from the end (see Diagram, page 147). Shape the handles by cutting with a jig saw, then sand the edges smooth.

Clamp the handles together and draw reference lines at the stringer locations.

When installing the stringers, make sure they are square with the handles.

3. Stringers and slats fit across the handles, creating the bottom frame of the porter. Clamp the handles together, edge to edge, so the ends are flush, and draw reference lines $25\frac{3}{8}$" from the grip ends and $3\frac{1}{2}$" from the square ends to locate the stringers (**photo A**). Place the front stringer flat across the bottom edges of the handles so the front edge of the stringer is flush with the $3\frac{1}{2}$" reference lines. Attach it with glue and $2\frac{1}{2}$" deck screws. Position the rear stringer between the handles so the back face of the stringer is flush with the $25\frac{3}{8}$" reference lines. Attach it with glue and $2\frac{1}{2}$" deck screws (**photo B**).

4. Cut the slats (J) to length, and round over their top edges with a sander.

5. Position the handle assembly so the shaped grip edges face down. Lay one slat over the handles at the front end so the corners of the slat are flush with the ends of the handles. Drill $\frac{1}{8}$" pilot holes through the slat, and counterbore the holes to a $\frac{1}{4}$" depth. Fasten the slat with glue and 2" deck screws.

6. Notch the rear end slat to receive the rear short stiles. Draw lines at both ends of the slat $\frac{7}{8}$" from a common long edge and $3\frac{1}{2}$" from the ends. Cut the notches with a jig saw. Position the slat flush with the rear face of the rear stringer, and fasten it with glue and 2" screws.

7. Space the remaining slats evenly between the end slats with gaps of about $\frac{1}{2}$". Fasten them with glue and 2" screws.

Make the corners.
Join the stiles to make the corners, which will support the side rails and end gates.

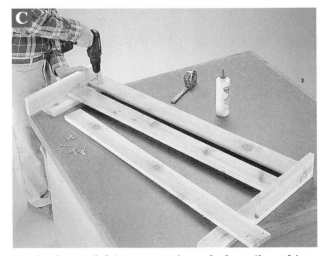

Apply glue and drive screws through the rails and into the corner pieces.

1. Cut the short stiles (D), long stiles (E) and rear stiles (F) to length. Use a compass to draw a 1¾"-radius semicircle at the bottom of each rear stile (see Diagram, page 147). Shape the ends with a jig saw, and sand the edges smooth.

2. Butt the edge of a short stile against the face of a rear stile so the pieces form a right angle. With the square ends flush, drill pilot holes every 2" through the rear stile and into the edge of the short stile. Counterbore the holes. Join the stiles with glue and 2" deck screws. Assemble the other rear corner.

3. Repeat this procedure to assemble the front corners, butting the edge of a long stile against the face of a short stile so the edges and tops are flush.

Make the sides.
1. Cut the side rails (I) to length. Place three side rails tight between one front corner and one rear corner so the top of the upper rail is flush with the tops of the corners. Leave a 1" gap between rails. Fasten the rails to the corners with glue and 1½" deck screws (**photo C**).

2. Fasten the side assemblies to the handles with glue and 2" deck screws (**photo D**). Drive an additional screw through each stile and into the edge of an adjacent slat. Position the remaining stiles (E) on the outer sides of the rails, midway between the front and rear corners. Fasten the stiles to the rails with glue and 1½" deck screws.

Make the gates.
1. Cut the gate stiles (G) and gate rails (H) to length. Sand the short edges of the rails.

2. Lay the rails facedown together in groups of

three with the ends flush. Draw reference lines across the rails 2" in from each end to locate the stiles.

3. Place two stiles on one rail with the tops flush and the outer stile edges on the reference lines. Fasten them with glue and 1½" deck screws driven through the stiles and into the rails.

4. Attach two more rails below the first one, leaving a 1" gap between the rails.

5. Follow the same procedure to make the other gate.

6. Set the gates in place between the porter sides to locate the four remaining gate stiles (G). These form the slots that keep the gates in place. Position the stiles flush with the tops of the top side rails and almost flush with the faces of the gate rails. Attach them with glue and 1½" deck screws driven through the stiles and into the rails. Slide the gates in and out of the slots to test for smooth operation.

7. Sand any rough areas, and apply the finish of your choice.

Attach the wheels.
1. Cut the axle to length (24" plus the width of the two wheels plus 1½"). Attach the axle to the bottom of the front stringer with lag screws and metal straps bent in the center (**photo E**). Place one strap at each end of the stringer and one in the middle.

2. Slide three washers followed by a wheel over each end of the axle. Secure the wheels with crimp caps or by drilling a small hole in each end of the axle and installing an additional washer and a cotter pin.

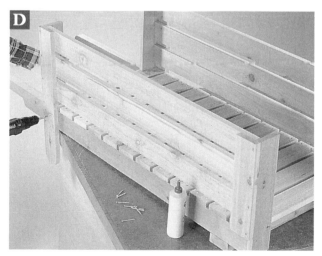

Anchor the sides to the framework with glue and screws driven through the stiles into the handles.

Attach the axles to the bottom of the front stringer with metal straps fastened with lag screws.

ADIRONDACK CHAIR

Adirondack furniture has become a standard on decks, porches and patios throughout the world. It's no mystery that this distinctive furniture style has become so popular. Attractive—but rugged—design and unmatched stability are just two of the reasons, and our Adirondack chair offers all of these benefits, and more.

But unlike most of the Adirondack chair designs available, this one is also very easy to build. There are no complex compound angles to cut, no intricate details on the back and seat slats, and no mortise-and-tenon joints. Like all of the projects in this book, our Adirondack chair can be built by any do-it-yourselfer, using basic tools and simple techniques. And because this design features all the elements of the classic Adirondack chair, your guests and neighbors may never guess that you built it yourself.

We made our Adirondack chair out of cedar and finished it with clear wood sealer. But you may prefer to build your version from pine (a traditional wood for Adirondack furniture), especially if you plan to paint the chair. White, battleship gray and forest green are popular color choices for Adirondack furniture. Be sure to use quality exterior paint with a glossy or enamel finish.

CONSTRUCTION MATERIALS

Quantity	Lumber
1	2 × 6" × 8' cedar
1	2 × 4" × 10' cedar
1	1 × 6" × 14' cedar
1	1 × 4" × 8' cedar
1	1 × 2" × 10' cedar

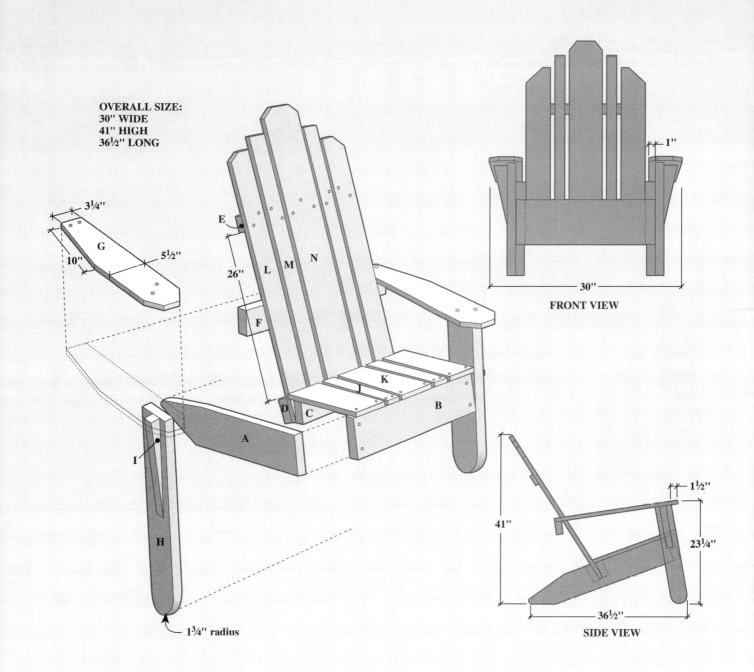

OVERALL SIZE:
30" WIDE
41" HIGH
36½" LONG

3¼"

G

10"

5½"

E

26"

L   M   N

F

D   C

K

B

A

I

H

1¾" radius

FRONT VIEW

30"

1"

SIDE VIEW

41"

36½"

1½"

23¼"

Cutting List				
Key	Part	Dimension	Pcs.	Material
A	Leg	1½ × 5½ × 34½"	2	Cedar
B	Apron	1½ × 5½ × 21"	1	Cedar
C	Seat support	1½ × 3½ × 18"	1	Cedar
D	Low back brace	1½ × 3½ × 18"	1	Cedar
E	High back brace	¾ × 1½ × 18"	1	Cedar
F	Arm cleat	1½ × 3½ × 24"	1	Cedar
G	Arm	¾ × 5½ × 28"	2	Cedar
H	Post	1½ × 3½ × 22"	2	Cedar

Cutting List				
Key	Part	Dimension	Pcs.	Material
I	Arm brace	1½ × 2¼ × 10"	2	Cedar
J	Narrow seat slat	¾ × 1½ × 20¼"	2	Cedar
K	Wide seat slat	¾ × 5½ × 20¼"	3	Cedar
L	End back slat	¾ × 3½ × 36"	2	Cedar
M	Narrow back slat	¾ × 1½ × 38"	2	Cedar
N	Center back slat	¾ × 5½ × 40"	1	Cedar

Materials: Moisture-resistant glue, 1¼", 1½", 2" and 3" deck screws, ⅜ × 2½" lag screws with washers, finishing materials.

Note: Measurements reflect the actual size of dimension lumber.

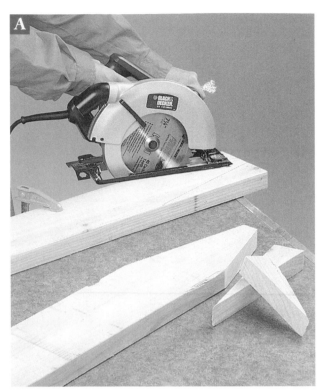

Cut tapers into the back edges of the legs.

Round the sharp slat edges with a router or a power sander.

HOW TO BUILD AN ADIRONDACK CHAIR

Cut the legs.

Sprawling back legs that support the seat slats and stretch to the ground on a near-horizontal plane are signature features of the Adirondack style.

1. Cut the legs (A) to length.

2. To make the tapers, mark a point on one end of the board, 2" from the edge. Then, mark another point on the adjacent edge, 6" from the end. Connect the points with a straightedge.

3. Mark a point on the same end, $2\frac{1}{4}$" in from the other edge. Then, mark a point on that edge, 10" from the end. Connect these points to make a cutting line for the other taper.

4. Cut the two taper cuts with a circular saw.

5. Use the tapered leg as a template to mark and cut identical tapers on the other leg of the chair (**photo A**).

Build the seat.

The legs form the sides of the box frame that supports the seat slats. Where counterbores for deck screws are called for, drill holes $\frac{1}{4}$" deep with a

counterbore bit.

1. Cut the apron (B) and seat support (C) to size.

2. Attach the apron to the front ends of the legs with glue and 3" deck screws, in the manner described above.

3. Position the seat support so the inside face is $16\frac{1}{2}$" from the inside edge of the apron. Attach the seat support between the legs, making sure the tops of the parts are flush.

4. Cut the seat slats (J) and (K) to length, and sand the ends smooth. Arrange the slats on top of the seat box, and use wood scraps to set $\frac{3}{8}$" spaces between the slats. The slats should overhang the front of the seat box by $\frac{3}{4}$".

5. Fasten the seat slats by drilling counterbored pilot holes and driving 2" deck screws through the holes and into the tops of the apron and seat support. Keep the counterbores aligned so the cedar plugs form straight lines across the front and back of the seat.

6. Once all the slats are installed, use a router with a $\frac{1}{4}$" roundover bit (or a power sander) to smooth the edges and ends of the slats (**photo B**).

Make decorative cuts on the fronts of the arms (shown) and the tops of the back slats, using a jig saw.

Make the back slats.
The back slats are made from three sizes of dimension lumber.

1. Cut the back slats (L), (M) and (N), to size.

2. Trim the corners on the wider slats. On the 1 × 6 slat (N), mark points 1" in from the outside, top corners. Then, mark points on the outside edges, 1" down from the corners. Connect the points and trim along the lines with a jig saw. Mark the 1 × 4 slats 2" from one top corner, in both directions. Draw cutting lines and trim.

Attach the back slats.
1. Cut the low back brace (D) and high back brace (E) and set them on a flat surface.

2. Slip ¾"-thick spacers under the high brace so the tops of the braces are level. Then, arrange the back slats on top of the braces with ⅝" spacing between slats. The untrimmed ends of the slats should be flush with the bottom edge of the low back brace. The bottom of the high back brace should be 26" above the top of the low brace. The braces must be perpendicular to the slats.

3. Drill pilot holes in the low brace and counterbore the holes. Then, attach the slats to the low

Attach the square ends of the posts to the undersides of the arms, being careful to position the part correctly.

brace by driving 2" deck screws through the holes. Follow the same steps for the high brace and attach the slats with 1¼" deck screws.

Cut the arms.
The broad arms of the chair are supported by posts in front, and a cleat attached to the backs of the chair slats.

1. Cut the arms (G) to size.

2. To create decorative angles at the outer end of each arm, mark points 1" from each corner along both edges. Use the points to draw a pair of 1½" cutting lines on each arm. Cut along the lines using a jig saw or circular saw **(photo C)**.

3. As an option, mark points for cutting a tapered cut on the inside, back edge of each arm (see Diagram). First, mark points on the back of each arm, 3¼" in from each inside edge. Next, mark the outside edges 10" from the back. Then, connect the points and cut the tapers with a circular saw or jig saw. Sand the edges smooth.

Assemble the arms, cleats and posts.

1. Cut the arm cleat (F) and make a mark $2\frac{1}{2}$" in from each end of the cleat.

2. Set the cleat on edge on your work surface. Position the arms on the top edge of the cleat so the back ends of the arms are flush with the back of the cleat and the untapered edge of each arm is aligned with the $2\frac{1}{2}$" mark. Fasten the arms to the cleats with glue.

3. Drill pilot holes in the arms and counterbore the holes. Drive 3" deck screws through the holes and into the cleat.

4. Cut the posts (H) to size. Then, use a compass to mark a $1\frac{3}{4}$"-radius roundover cut on each bottom post corner (the roundovers improve stability).

5. Position the arms on top of the square ends of the posts. The posts should be set back $1\frac{1}{2}$" from the front ends of the arm, and 1" from the inside edge of the arm. Fasten the arms to the posts with glue.

6. Drill pilot holes in the arms and counterbore the holes. Then, drive 3" deck screws through the arms and into the posts **(photo D)**.

7. Cut tapered arm braces (I) from wood scraps, making sure the grain of the wood runs lengthwise. Position an arm brace at the outside of each arm/post joint, centered side to side on the post. Attach each brace with glue.

8. Drill pilot holes in the inside face of the post near the top and counterbore the holes. Then, drive deck screws through the holes and into the brace **(photo E)**. Drive a 2" deck screw down through each arm and into the top of the brace.

Assemble the chair.

All that remains is to join the back, seat/leg assembly and arm/post assembly to complete construc-

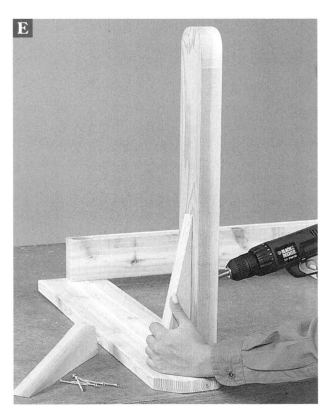

Drive screws through each post and into an arm brace to stabilize the arm/post joint.

Clamp wood braces to the parts of the chair to hold them in position while you fasten the parts together.

tion. Before you start, gather scrap wood to brace the parts while you fasten them.

1. Set the seat/leg assembly on your work surface, clamping a piece of scrap wood to the front apron to raise the front of the assembly until the bottoms of the legs are flush on the surface (about 10").

2. Use a similar technique to brace the arm/post assembly so the bottom of the back cleat is 20" above the work surface. Arrange the assembly so the posts fit around the front of the seat/leg assembly, and the bottom edge of the apron is flush with the front edges of the posts.

3. Drill a ¼"-dia. pilot hole through the inside of each leg and partway into the post. Drive a ³⁄₈ × 2½" lag screw and washer through each hole, but do not tighten completely (**photo F**). Remove the braces.

4. Position the back so the low back brace is between the legs, and the slats are resting against the front of the arm cleat. Clamp the back to the seat support with a C-clamp, making sure the top edge of the low brace is flush with the tops of the legs.

5. Tighten the lag screws at the post/leg joints. Then, add a second lag screw at each joint.

6. Drill three evenly spaced pilot holes near the top edge of the arm cleat and drive 1½" deck screws through the holes and into the back slats (**photo G**). Drive 3" deck screws through the legs and into the ends of the low back brace.

Apply finishing touches.
1. Glue ¼"-thick, ³⁄₈"-dia. cedar wood plugs into visible counterbores (**photo H**).

2. After the glue dries, sand the plugs even with the surrounding surface. Finish-sand all exposed surfaces with 120-grit sandpaper.

3. Finish the chair as desired—we simply applied a coat of clear wood sealer.

Drive screws through the arm cleat, near the top, and into the slats.

Glue cedar plugs into the counterbores to conceal the screw holes.

CONVERSION CHARTS

Converting Measurements

To Convert:	To:	Multiply by:
Inches	Millimeters	25.4
Inches	Centimeters	2.54
Feet	Meters	0.305
Yards	Meters	0.914
Square inches	Square centimeters	6.45
Square feet	Square meters	0.093
Square yards	Square meters	0.836
Cubic inches	Cubic centimeters	16.4
Cubic feet	Cubic meters	0.0283
Cubic yards	Cubic meters	0.765
Ounces	Milliliters	30.0
Pints (U.S.)	Liters	0.473 (lmp. 0.568)
Quarts (U.S.)	Liters	0.946 (lmp. 1.136)
Gallons (U.S.)	Liters	3.785 (lmp. 4.546)
Ounces	Grams	28.4
Pounds	Kilograms	0.454

To Convert:	To:	Multiply by:
Millimeters	Inches	0.039
Centimeters	Inches	0.394
Meters	Feet	3.28
Meters	Yards	1.09
Square centimeters	Square inches	0.155
Square meters	Square feet	10.8
Square meters	Square yards	1.2
Cubic centimeters	Cubic inches	0.061
Cubic meters	Cubic feet	35.3
Cubic meters	Cubic yards	1.31
Milliliters	Ounces	.033
Liters	Pints (U.S.)	2.114 (lmp. 1.76)
Liters	Quarts (U.S.)	1.057 (lmp. 0.88)
Liters	Gallons (U.S.)	0.264 (lmp. 0.22)
Grams	Ounces	0.035
Kilograms	Pounds	2.2

Lumber Dimensions

Nominal - U.S.	Actual - U.S.	METRIC
1 × 2	¾ × 1½"	19 × 38 mm
1 × 3	¾ × 2½"	19 × 64 mm
1 × 4	¾ × 3½"	19 × 89 mm
1 × 5	¾ × 4½"	19 × 114 mm
1 × 6	¾ × 5½"	19 × 140 mm
1 × 7	¾ × 6¼"	19 × 159 mm
1 × 8	¾ × 7¼"	19 × 184 mm
1 × 10	¾ × 9¼"	19 × 235 mm
1 × 12	¾ × 11¼"	19 × 286 mm
1¼ × 4	1 × 3½"	25 × 89 mm
1¼ × 6	1 × 5½"	25 × 140 mm
1¼ × 8	1 × 7¼"	25 × 184 mm
1¼ × 10	1 × 9¼"	25 × 235 mm
1¼ × 12	1 × 11¼"	25 × 286 mm

Nominal - U.S.	Actual - U.S.	METRIC
1½ × 4	1¼ × 3½"	32 × 89 mm
1½ × 6	1¼ × 5½"	32 × 140 mm
1½ × 8	1¼ × 7¼"	32 × 184 mm
1½ × 10	1¼ × 9¼"	32 × 235 mm
1½ × 12	1¼ × 11¼"	32 × 286 mm
2 × 4	1½ × 3½"	38 × 89 mm
2 × 6	1½ × 5½"	38 × 140 mm
2 × 8	1½ × 7¼"	38 × 184 mm
2 × 10	1½ × 9¼"	38 × 235 mm
2 × 12	1½ × 11¼"	38 × 286 mm
3 × 6	2½ × 5½"	64 × 140 mm
4 × 4	3½ × 3½"	89 × 89 mm
4 × 6	3½ × 5½"	89 × 140 mm

PHOTO CREDITS

INDEX

A

Adirondack chair project, 150–155
Air cleaners, servicing, 40
Animal pests, 24
  bats, 56–58
  bears, 54, 62, 63–66
  checking for, 35
  deer, 66–67
  law and, 53–54
  mice, 44–45, 47, 54–56, 119–120
  porcupines, 60–61, 63
  raccoons, 59–60
  shutdown and, 87
  skunks, 58–59
  squirrels, 56
Appliance shutdown, 118

B

Basement problems, 91–93
Bats, 56–58
Batteries, 41
Bears, 54, 62, 63–66
Boats, 39, 41
Brick stains, 92
Building codes, 17–18

C

Cabin marker project, 142–145
Cabin porter project, 146–149
Cabin rules, 84–85
Checklists
  for guests, 89
  for opening, 34–35, 48–49
  for shutdown, 121
Chimney maintenance, 93–95
Communication issues, 77–78, 84–85
Conflict resolution, 78, 81

D

Damper inspection, 93
Deer, 66–67
Dock box project, 138–141
Dock installation, 41–42, 44
Dock shutdown procedure, 118
Double-hung windows, weatherstripping, 30

E

Electrical power, 120–121

F

Firebox, 120
Fire pit project, 126–129
Fires, 100, 112–113
Firewood
    shed project, 130–137
    supply, 46–47, 75, 99–101
Flue inspection, 93
Food
    purchases, 47, 78–79
    shutdown and, 47, 87, 119

G

Garbage shed project, 130–137
Gas-powered tools, 39
Guests, 83–89

H

Handymen, 79
Heating system
    firewood for, 46–47, 75, 99–101
    guests and, 85
    maintenance, 93–95
Home types, 27–29, 31
Hunting, 80–81

I

Insect pests, 66–69

K

Keys, 85

L

Landscaping, 103–105, 108–113
Lawns, 103–105, 108–110
Loose-fill pathway project, 106–107

M

Maintenance
    attitudes toward, 9–13
    preventive, 12–13
    schedules, 38
Mice, 44–45, 47, 54–56, 119–120
Mildew, 91–93
Motors, 39, 41

O

Opening weekend
    cleanup, 44–45
    plan, 34–35
Ownership reasons, 7–8, 11–12

P

Pathway projects
    loose-fill, 106–107
    stepping stone, 124–125
Porch steps project, 20–23
Porcupines, 60–61, 63
Pumps, 37, 96
Purchases, 78–79

R

Raccoons, 59–60
Residents, year-round, 72–81
Resupply, 45–48

S

Security, 19, 24
    neighbors and, 79–80
    shutdown and, 88
    during winter, 120, 121
Septic systems
    described, 17
    location, 109–110
    maintaining, 97, 98–99
    during winter, 119
Shoreline maintenance, 103–105, 108–110
Shutdown procedures
    final for season, 115–122
    guests and, 86–88

Skunks, 58–59
Small engine maintenance, 38, 39–40, 43, 119
Spark plugs, 43
Squirrels, 56
Stepping stone pathway project, 124–125

T

Trees, 110–112, 118–119
Trespass, 80–81

W

Walkway projects
    loose-fill, 106–107
    stepping stone, 124–125
Water systems
    pumps, 37, 96
    shutdown, 116–117
    start-up, 36, 39
    well maintenance, 95–96, 98
Weather issues, 18–19, 74, 115–121
Well maintenance, 37, 95–96, 98
Windows, weatherstripping double-hung, 30
Wooden porch steps project, 20–23

Also from

CREATIVE PUBLISHING INTERNATIONAL

IdeaWise Activity Spaces
IdeaWise Basements & Attics
IdeaWise Bathrooms
IdeaWise Decks & Patios
IdeaWise Garages
IdeaWise Kitchens
IdeaWise Porches & Sunrooms
IdeaWise Storage
IdeaWise Yards & Gardens

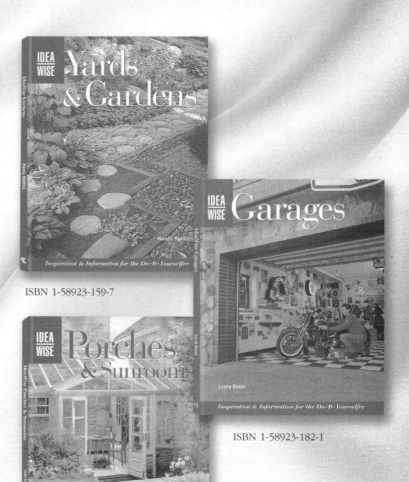

ISBN 1-58923-159-7

ISBN 1-58923-182-1

ISBN 1-58923-223-2

CREATIVE PUBLISHING INTERNATIONAL

18705 LAKE DRIVE EAST
CHANHASSEN, MN 55317

WWW.CREATIVEPUB.COM

07/06

Complete Guide to Bathrooms
Complete Guide to Building Decks
Complete Guide to Ceramic & Stone Tile
Complete Guide to Creative Landscapes
Complete Guide to Easy Woodworking Projects
Complete Guide to Flooring
Complete Guide to Home Carpentry
Complete Guide to Home Masonry
Complete Guide to Home Plumbing
Complete Guide to Home Storage
Complete Guide to Home Wiring
Complete Guide to Kitchens
Complete Guide to Outdoor Wood Projects
Complete Guide to Painting & Decorating
Complete Guide to Roofing & Siding
Complete Guide to Windows & Doors
Complete Guide to Yard & Garden Features
Complete Photo Guide to Home Repair
Complete Photo Guide to Home Improvement
Complete Photo Guide to Outdoor Home Repair

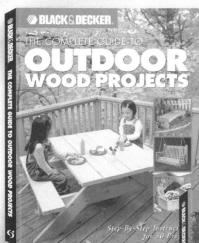

ISBN 1-58923-202-X

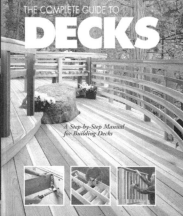

ISBN 1-58923-200-3

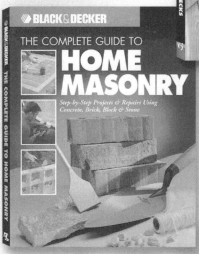

ISBN 0-86573-592-1

CREATIVE PUBLISHING INTERNATIONAL

18705 LAKE DRIVE EAST
CHANHASSEN, MN 55317
WWW.CREATIVEPUB.COM